Literature in Perspective

General Editor: Kenneth H. Grose

Joseph Conrad

Literature in Perspective

Joseph Conrad

Neville H. Newhouse

Evans Brothers Limited, London

Published by Evans Brothers Limited
Montague House, Russell Square, London, W.C.1.
© Neville H. Newhouse 1966
First published 1966

PR6005
.046 Z784

Set in 11 on 12 point Fournier and printed in Great Britain by
C. Tinling & Co. Ltd., Liverpool, London and Prescot
7/5317   PR3615

Literature in Perspective

Of recent years, the ordinary man who reads for pleasure has been gradually excluded from that great debate in which every intelligent reader of the classics takes part. There are two reasons for this: first, so much criticism floods from the world's presses that no one but a scholar living entirely among books can hope to read it all; and second, the critics and analysts, mostly academics, use a language that only their fellows in the same discipline can understand.

Consequently criticism, which should be as 'inevitable as breathing'—an activity for which we are all qualified—has become the private field of a few warring factions who shout their unintelligible battle cries to each other but make little communication to the common man.

Literature in Perspective aims at giving a straightforward account of literature and of writers—straightforward both in content and in language. Critical jargon is as far as possible avoided; any terms that must be used are explained simply; and the constant preoccupation of the authors of the Series is to be lucid.

It is our hope that each book will be easily understood, that it will adequately describe its subject without pretentiousness so that the intelligent reader who wants to know about Donne or Keats or Shakespeare will find enough in it to bring him up to date on critical estimates.

Even those who are well read, we believe, can benefit from a lucid exposition of what they may have taken for granted, and perhaps—dare it be said?—not fully understood.   K. H. G.

Joseph Conrad

Conrad is a difficult and uneven writer. I have tried in this book to do no more than indicate some simple lines of approach to his more important novels and stories.

I have used the Dent Collected Edition of Conrad's Works, 1950 (including *A Personal Record*), to which all chapter and page numbers refer. Relevant editions of all other titles quoted from can be found in the Bibliography at the end of this book. The name Baines indicates a reference to this author's standard critical biography of Conrad (1960), and the name Gordan a reference to *Joseph Conrad. The Making of a Novelist* (1940).

I wish to thank my friend and editor, Mr. Kenneth Grose, for his generous encouragement and advice.

N. H. N.

Contents

The Author

Neville H. Newhouse, M.A., is the Headmaster of Friends' School, Lisburn, County Antrim.

Acknowledgements

The author and publishers are indebted to the following for permission to use illustrations and quotations: J. M. Dent & Sons Ltd. and the Trustees of the Joseph Conrad Estate for extracts from the Works of Conrad and *Joseph Conrad: Life and Letters*, (Heinemann, 1927), edited by G. Jean-Aubry, and for the photograph of the young Conrad and facsimile of the page from *Nostromo*, both appearing in the above mentioned book; David Higham Associates Ltd. and Mrs. Theodora Zavin for the quotations from *Joseph Conrad: A Personal Rememberance*, by Ford Madox Ford; The Nautical Photo Agency, Suffolk, for the photograph of the 'Otago'; The Mansell Collection for the photograph of Jacob Epstein's bust of Conrad; and Paul Popper Ltd. for the cover picture of Conrad.

I

Conrad's Life

This book will be about what Conrad wrote, not about his life. Yet it will begin with a short biography. This is not because Conrad's life is interesting in itself (as it is), nor because it will give a clearer picture of Conrad the man (as it should do), but because it may help to throw light on our main concern—the themes of the novels and the manner of their treatment. And it seems fair to say that, in the consideration of any work of art, this is the most profitable use of biographical material. We shall not understand Shakespeare's sonnets any better even if, as seems highly unlikely, we do establish the identity of the dark lady; no more do we need to know who Doña Rita or Kurtz were in real life, in order to appreciate and evaluate *The Arrow of Gold* and *Heart of Darkness*.

SOURCES FOR CONRAD'S LIFE

There are three sources for Conrad's life: his own autobiographical statements, his novels, and the writings of others (both contemporaries and later scholars) about the things Conrad did. The first of these must be treated with care. After all, as an artist Conrad moulded events in order to construct novels. Why should he not have done this even in *A Personal Record*? Again, like anyone else, he must have suffered from lapses of memory and distorting prejudices. These lead all of us to plain mis-statements of fact, although it is often difficult to establish such mistakes.

The second source is unreliable, and there is a danger in even considering it biographically. But Conrad was the kind of novelist who found his material in the people and events of his early life and sailing days (not like, say, the Orwell of *1984*, where the situations cannot stem from his own life). For those who wish to explore the way in which memories can be translated into art, Conrad offers a rich field for examination.

It is the third source, the writings of others, that is the most dependable. Conrad's own friends, his wife, and Ford Madox Ford, in particular, reveal him vividly, but in a highly personal way. And though scholars disagree about some of the details of Conrad's life story, they have established beyond doubt its main outlines. These are here set down.

POLAND AND FRANCE

It is important to stress, first, Conrad's foreignness. English novelist he may have been, but as a boy he lived in a great gloomy house set in the endless, undulating plains of the Ukraine, a bleak background matching the tragedy of his early years. His distinguished Polish family had no fatherland and both before and after Conrad's birth in 1857, lost wealth and life for Poland, particularly at the hands of Russia, the most cruel of the partitioning powers. It was for his father's work as a leader of the revolutionary movement against Russia that his parents were exiled to Northern Russia. His mother died when he was eight, his father four years later, in 1869. Twice Conrad became familiar with the awful stillness of the sickroom and with gliding nuns who, austere in their black gowns and cloistral in their whispers, instilled into him the resignation of imminent death.

One immediate result of this sombre childhood was that he became a great reader. His father (Korzeniowski was his name) was something of a scholar, and translated both Shakespeare and Victor Hugo into Polish. During his last illness he got his son to read aloud to him the proofs of some of his work. So it was early in his life that Conrad became familiar with the mechanics of writing and publishing. And during his long, lonely and unoccupied hours he turned to his father's library. At the age of five, he began reading, in Polish and in French, history, voyages and novels. If his own memory is to be trusted, he had tackled Hugo, Cervantes, Dickens, Scott and Thackeray by the time he was ten.

He now came under the guardianship of Tadeusz Brobowski, an uncle on his mother's side, and, after a year or so at school, expressed a wish to go to sea. Disapproving, Uncle Tadeusz did his best to dissuade him. He sent him on a continental holiday with a tutor whose instructions were to turn the boy's interests elsewhere. A short section of *A Personal Record* tells us the outcome, and offers us a glimpse of Conrad's method of handling his memories. The tutor argued continually and with dogged perseverance. By the time the two had reached the top of the Furca Pass, he was perhaps not far from success. Just then a sturdy Englishman, clad in knickerbockers and short socks, strode past. Conrad noticed his 'headlong, exalted satisfaction' and 'his innocently eager and triumphant eyes'. The sight enabled Conrad to pull himself together, and he was able to renew his defence of himself. Quite suddenly the tutor rose, saying: 'You are an incorrigible Don Quixote. That's what you are.' The two walked on in silence. Then, as the shadows lengthened and the mountains grew blacker, the tutor put his hand on the boy's shoulder, remarking: 'Well! That's enough. We will have no more of it' (40–5).

Is it rather fanciful, this dramatised moment? Did the Englishman really have anything to do with the decision to go to sea, or is he one of Conrad's conscious symbols, given later a significance which he was far from possessing at the time? It does not matter. The point is that, recorded like this, it brings home to the reader the determination of a frail, sad and lonely boy. The novels often work like this, too, heightening and isolating incidents from Conrad's youth.

Conrad had his way, and one September day in 1874, still not quite seventeen and 'like a man in a dream', he left Vienna for Marseilles. About his three-and-a-half years in France there is debate. His own accounts of them in *The Arrow of Gold* and *The Mirror of the Sea* are highly romantic. They are (to speak with our symbolic Englishman still in mind) a long succession of glamorously heightened incidents. Writing of them over thirty years later, Conrad tried to invest them with magic (his own word). But some things are clear enough. For several months he did not undertake serious seamanship, and was content to work vaguely alongside the volatile and noisy Provençal pilots and sailors. Then he made a trip to the West Indies. It was on this voyage that he met Dominic, the second mate, who greatly influenced Conrad's attitude to sailing and to life.

Dominic seems to have been unfailingly loyal to his friends and to his duty as a sailor, but he showed scant respect for the lawful authorities of the earth. For eighteen months he and Conrad were inseparable. They supplied contraband arms to rebel troops in both the West Indies and Spain. Then Dominic left Conrad, apparently after their betrayal by Dominic's nephew. Conrad, meantime, had lost his heart to a wealthy young woman much implicated in the activities of the Carlist Pretender to the Spanish throne. For a short time they lived together in the Maritime Alps, an affair brought to a sudden end by her leaving him, possibly after he had fought a duel on her behalf. The details are obscure, and differing suggestions can be found in Conrad's biographers. What is certain is that Doña Rita, as he called her, provided Conrad with an idyll which greatly influenced his art. 'They were', he wrote in *The Arrow of Gold*, 'companions who had found out each other's fitness in a specially intense way' (338). As soon as the affair with her was over, Conrad embarked on an English steamer bound for Constantinople. It brought him back from there to Lowestoft.

THE BRITISH MERCHANT SERVICE

The next eight years of his life are the story of the fulfilment of what he claimed was a boyhood determination to be 'an English seaman worthy of the service'. He seems to have been aware that he owed it to himself, to the memory of his parents and to his uncle to succeed, and when, at the end of the eight years in 1886, he was both a qualified master in the Mercantile Marine and a naturalised Englishman, he had fully accomplished his intentions. In doing so, he had made two voyages to Australia, two to China and two shorter trips to Italy and India.

On the evidence of *A Personal Record*, one would think that this remarkable success was the result of the pursuit of a single-minded objective—that Conrad had first deliberately chosen to be a British sailor, had next spent a little time on the way sowing wild oats in the South of France and in the West Indies, and had finally set about making his career in an undeviatingly purposeful way. In fact, it was not at all like that. It was not without many backward glances, and several attempts to leave his vocation altogether, that Conrad eventually arrived at the point where he was qualified to captain a ship. He thought of returning to the Ukraine; then to Marseilles; of going to Canada as secretary to a business man; of setting off (as late as 1885) on a whaling expedition. As it happened none of these schemes came to anything, but they were all seriously discussed with other people. And this fact is of interest here in two ways—it shows that we cannot take Conrad's autobiographical writing at its face value; and it underlines a common theme of the novels, namely that a man is what his life has made him, rather than the captain of his fate and master of his soul.

A number of Conrad's essays record his estimate of the effect on him of the Merchant Service. In general, he was rarely seduced into a romantic attitude towards it. Early in his career as a sailor he took a boat to the rescue of nine Danes stranded in mid-Atlantic, an experience which enabled him to look 'coolly at the life of my choice. Its illusions were gone, but its fascination remained'. There seems to have been a sense in which Conrad thought of the sea as Melville's Captain Ahab thought of the white whale, Moby Dick: as an enemy with whom no truce was possible. In combating the enemy a high degree of skill was necessary, especially in sailing vessels (as opposed to steamships), and all the evidence points to the fact that Conrad was himself a skilful sailor. The very fact that sailing was an art seemed to him to make demands upon men and to call out special qualities in them. It was not that sailors were better individual men than any other craftsmen; but by the nature of their work they were bound together in close fellowship and dedicated to honest efficiency—for 'no ship navigated and sailed in the happy-go-lucky manner people conduct their business on shore would ever arrive in port'. Life on shipboard was a special life and demanded total loyalty and discipline, not from compulsion but from a sense of the finest traditions of the calling. One of the purposes of Conrad's life was to find and serve a persisting reality which would outlast the merely fleeting aspect of the lives of individual men.

It is not clear why Conrad gave up his captaincy of a ship plying between Sydney and Mauritius. It has been suggested that a young lady in that island refused his offer of marriage. But whether or not this is so, it is certainly true that it was while he was trying to gain another command that he began his first novel, *Almayer's Folly*. It was now that he undertook his last captaincy—of a steamship which went up the Congo into the heart of the African jungle. This trip was virtually the end of his life as a sailor. It had also great significance in forming the themes and statements of his art. Much later in life he said that until he visited Africa in 1890 he was 'just a mere animal'. He meant by these words that he experienced in Africa a peculiarly intense insight into the possibilities of evil in man. His most direct testimony of the vision is his story, *Heart of Darkness*.

LITERARY CAREER

If Conrad's achievement in becoming a captain in the British Merchant Service is remarkable, his achievement in becoming a great English novelist is far more so. It is one thing simply to write a few books; it is quite another to aim at and to achieve greatness in an art form.

He first turned to writing from a number of causes. For one thing, his father had done literary work, and, naturally enough, he himself 'liked taking up a pen' (as early as 1886 he had sent a short story to the magazine *Titbits*); then, he found he could not obtain another command (after Africa he made only two more voyages, both colourless and both to Australia as First Officer on a modern vessel); and, finally, his health broke down. He thus found time hanging heavy on his hands, and he also needed money to support himself.

Conrad has told us that he began *Almayer's Folly* in a vague, blundering sort of way. 'Never had Rubicon been more blindly forded, without invocation to the gods, without fear of men' (*A Personal Record*, 69). The general truth of this is borne out by scholars who have studied the manuscript of Conrad's first novel. The many corrections show that for a long time after starting it, Conrad had no idea of how it would turn out. It was as though his characters ruled him, themselves suggesting turns of the plot which he followed without asking where they led. In this way, although Conrad took the liberty of using acquaintances as starting-points for many of his novels, he need hardly have apologised for doing so, because they soon exploited him and shaped his texts for him. This was one of the reasons, as he admits in the Author's Note to his second novel, why he continued writing: the experience was new to him and he surrendered himself to the delights of his own imagination.

From now on Conrad's life became much less colourful. Luckily, the manuscript of *Almayer's Folly* came before Edward Garnett, then a young reader for Fisher Unwin, the London publishers. Throughout his life this son of a scholarly keeper of the British Museum encouraged new authors. 'How much you have done to pull me together intellectually', Conrad told Garnett in 1923, just a year before his own death, 'only the Goods that brought us together know' (Gordan, 307). Another loyal and generous friend was John Galsworthy (Garnett watched over him, too). Then there was Henry James. Conrad sent him a presentation copy of *An Outcast of the Islands* and received in return *The Spoils of Poynton*. There followed regular visits between the two, although the friendship never became close. Their elaborate courtesies were a source of amusement to some observers. Other friends were W. E. Henley, now remembered chiefly as a very minor poet, but then an important figure on the literary scene; Stephen Crane, the American author of *The Red Badge of Courage*, a Civil War story in which the glories of the fight were replaced by an insistence on retreat and squalid misery; R. Cunninghame Graham, a romantic knight-errant who eventually took up the cause of socialism and worked alongside such pioneers as Morris, Hyndman, Shaw and Keir Hardie; and H. G. Wells, who left some reminiscences of Conrad.

But of all the writers with whom Conrad now spent his very different life, far the most important was Ford Madox Hueffer, known today as Ford Madox Ford. He was a difficult man, opinionated and patronising (Crane said that when he got to Heaven, Ford would patronise God Almighty Himself). But he was very able. He collaborated with Conrad in *Romance*, and the two spent hours together discussing their art. Ford eventually wrote a series of novels about the Great War (the Tietjens novels), and ended up in America, where as a literary critic he influenced the taste of the day. It is very likely that his novels will at length be accorded more recognition, and that some day there will be a critical assessment of his particular influence on Conrad. In the end the two men quarrelled and separated.

Conrad had married in 1896. The story of his courtship has been recorded by his wife. Of no special interest in itself, it all seems to have been remarkably humourless. Indeed, Conrad's married life was often highly odd, and its oddity began with his proposal. He spent a long morning with the lady of his choice in the National Gallery, in the course of which he formally proposed marriage. He was in considerable haste, arguing that the ceremony ought to take place within one or two weeks as the weather was bad and he feared he had not long to live. After lunch, he escorted Jessie George home in a cab, sitting by her in complete silence for almost an hour. Three days later he summoned Jessie and her mother to an evening meal, at which he repeated his earlier urgencies, adding to the fact that he had not long to live, the determination to have no children. Immediate marriage was therefore, he said, imperative!

Thus began the partnership in which Jessie George found

herself faced with regular removals (removals demanded by Conrad himself but organised by her, since he went to stay with friends while she supervised the unloading of vans and the positioning of furniture as well as she could); faced, too, with endless debts (for even after he had achieved fame and good money he squandered his wealth); and with such idiosyncrasies as his sudden decision to work at his books nowhere save in the bathroom. A full account of all this domestic strangeness can be read in the two books which Jessie Conrad wrote about him.

Marriage and the birth of sons in 1898 and 1906 necessarily meant more responsibility, and it became increasingly urgent for Conrad to make more money by his writing. This he found very hard to do. Although by the turn of the century he was well established as a writer and had won a large circle of literary friends, it was only with extreme difficulty that he made ends meet. He drove himself harder; his books became longer and more ambitious, and the writing of them ever more laborious. From 1900 to the outbreak of the 1914–18 war, Conrad's life was almost entirely given over to his writing, the only interruptions being illness and occasional continental holidays. And all the time he sought both recognition and literary excellence. Wells said that Conrad went 'literary with a singleness and intensity of purpose that made the kindred concentration of Henry James seem lax and large and pale'; and Ford praised in him the 'strong faith that in our day and hour the writing of novels is the only pursuit worth while for a proper man'.

Conrad pinned his faith in *Nostromo* (1904), his most complicated and in many ways his most impressive novel. When it went unacclaimed, he was bitterly disappointed. Reviewers, he concluded, were to blame for this state of affairs—they lacked discrimination. To them, *Nostromo* was no different from the much slighter, earlier works, while *Typhoon* was just a short sea-tale, interesting for a few vivid descriptions.

Nevertheless, by 1911 there were clear signs that Conrad's work was making its way into the world. An essay appeared in French on Conrad's art; an American collector paid £30 for the script of *An Outcast*; in the summer of 1911, Conrad was granted a yearly pension of £100 on the Civil List for Services to Literature; and there was a contract for a serial with the *New York Herald*. Then in 1913, *Chance* became a best-seller. Conrad's literary agent (who had stood loyally by him during the lean years) was able to conclude some very profitable bargains for him. Even while Conrad was still writing *Victory* (the next book after *Chance*), he knew it would bring him at least £2,000.

Then came the Great War. From the public hysteria of the Boer War, Conrad had held aloof; Kipling's assertion that it was a war undertaken for the cause of democracy, had drawn from him the withering comment, '*C'est à crever de rire*' (I could die laughing). In 1914 he adopted no such sceptical attitude. Why was this, in one whose art was deeply questioning, particularly of the political world? There must have been many reasons, but one very likely one was his elder son's participation. Astonishingly, too, Conrad, invited by the Admiralty at the age of sixty to visit ports and inspect the work of the R.N.V.R., found himself in an old sailing ship hunting submarines in the North Sea. It was the briefest of episodes. He returned to his writing and in *The Arrow of Gold* produced quite his worst novel. As the war drew to a close, all his scepticism returned. He 'begged to be excused from the public ecstasies of joy' at the 1917 Russian Revolution, and he watched with gloom and alarm the post-war fate of his native Poland. He did not believe that either conciliation with Russia or the universal peace of President Wilson (who conceived the League of Nations) were possible. Cunninghame Graham, the idealistic socialist, was, he noted, enthusiastically pursuing all kinds of idealistic projects, in the 'unwarrantable belief' that they could ever be realised. For his part, his interest centred itself round the fortunes of his books, though he also watched closely the fate of his native Poland. He returned in *The Rescue* to the early themes and characters of his first two novels. In *The Rover* he once more produced a slighter tale (a little longer than *Typhoon* but with the same strict control). And all the time his literary fame grew. It reached its highest point during his lifetime in 1923 when manuscripts, the equivalent of which he had been glad enough in his early days to sell for thirty or forty pounds, realised £4,000 in New York. Even in England 'the reverberation in the press is very great indeed, and the result is that lots of people, who never heard of me before, now know my name, and thousands of others, who could not have read through a page of mine without falling into convulsions, are proclaiming me a very great author'. The ironic tone speaks for itself. He was not deceived. 'Perhaps you won't find it presumption', he once said, 'if, after twenty-two years of work, I may say that I have not been very well understood'.

His death came suddenly from a heart attack. As he was lowered into his grave in Canterbury cemetery, the festivities of the cricket week were in full swing. 'Suddenly', said Virginia Woolf, 'without giving us time to arrange our thoughts or prepare our phrases, our guest has left us: and his withdrawal without farewell or ceremony is in keeping with his mysterious arrival, long years ago, to take up lodging in this country'.

It is difficult to picture so varied a man. Among his characteristics were determination, capacity for hard work, and loyalty to his friends and principles. On the other hand, unfitted by his unusual youth and his life as a sailor for domesticity, he was often selfish, testy and unreasonable. It does not matter. For such a man it is the inner life, the questing of the spirit, that is important. Conrad's vivid imagination, together with his unyielding pessimism about the social and political future of man, condemned him to a fundamental loneliness. Out of it were born novels. And though Conrad the novelist, not the man, is to be our concern, it needs saying that always the whole man is greater than his skill, however great that may be. Surprisingly, it is the cool and rational Bertrand Russell who has left us perhaps the best impression of the force of Conrad's personality. It is an account of their first meeting and may be found in *Portraits from Memory*:

> We talked with increasing intimacy. We seemed to sink through layer after layer of what was superficial, till gradually both reached the central fire. It was an experience unlike any other

that I have known. We looked into each other's eyes, half appalled and half intoxicated to find ourselves together in such a region. The emotion was intense as passionate love, and at the same time all-embracing. I came away bewildered, and hardly able to find my way among ordinary affairs.   84

2

Literary Background

The listing and dating of Conrad's works is not quite as simple as might be expected. Some were published in book form; some were published serially and did not appear as books until later, occasionally with considerable differences as in *The Secret Agent*; often two or three were being written at the same time; and there were many articles and short stories. But if we confine our attention to the main novels, dating them by their first appearance, then the list is made up as follows:

1895 *Almayer's Folly*
1896 *An Outcast of the Islands*
1897 *The Nigger of the Narcissus*
1898 *Youth*
1899 *Heart of Darkness*
1900 *Lord Jim*
1902 *Typhoon*
1903 *Romance* (jointly with Ford Madox Ford)
1904 *Nostromo*
1906 *The Mirror of the Sea*
1907 *The Secret Agent*
1911 *Under Western Eyes*
1912 *Chance*
1915 *Victory*
1916 *The Shadow Line*
1919 *The Arrow of Gold*
1919 *The Rescue* (started in 1896, then discontinued)
1923 *The Rover*
1925 *Suspense* (unfinished)

Conrad's first novel, then, was published in 1895. What was the literary scene which he so surprisingly entered?

The great age of the Victorian novel was over. Thackeray had died in 1863, Dickens in 1870, George Eliot in 1880 and Trollope in 1882. Meredith and Hardy were still living, but neither published a novel after 1895. Who, then, was writing at the turn of the century?

Here is a short list of novels with their dates of publication:

1897	*Captains Courageous*	very late Kipling
	The Spoils of Poynton	fairly late Henry James
1898	*Jocelyn*	Galsworthy's first novel
1900	*Love and Mr. Lewisham*	early H. G. Wells
1902	*Anna of the Five Towns*	very early Arnold Bennett

Of these names, Henry James is clearly the most important; standard histories of the English novel usually consider Kipling, Galsworthy, Wells and Bennett to be less serious artists.

Twenty years later, a comparable list reads as follows:

1918	*Tarr*	Wyndham Lewis's first novel
1921	*Crome Yellow*	Aldous Huxley's first novel
	To Let	Galsworthy in the middle of *The Forsyte Saga*
1922	*Ulysses*	James Joyce
1923	*Kangaroo*	D. H. Lawrence in mid-career
	Riceyman Steps	late Bennett
1924	*Passage to India*	E. M. Forster's last novel
	Some do not	late Ford Madox Ford
1925	*Mrs. Dalloway*	Virginia Woolf in mid-career
1926	*The World of William Clissold*	late H. G. Wells

This is a very different list from the first. Its most important name is James Joyce, an innovator in a sense in which Galsworthy, Wells and Bennett (the only names in both lists) are clearly not. It seems odd, too, to think of Conrad writing at the same time as Lawrence, Joyce and Virginia Woolf. They are more 'modern', as we like to say.

From Dickens to Joyce is a long way and it is obvious that *Ulysses* (1922) is a very different novel from *A Tale of Two Cities* (1859). One of the very many differences is particularly important in this context. It has been well described by J. Warren Beach in his *The Twentieth Century Novel* (1932).

Instead of making the reader feel for himself the poignancy and dramatic power of a scene, Victorian novelists announce the emotions that the reader ought to be experiencing. In so doing, the novelists intrude themselves between the reader and the story. And Warren Beach notes three major tendencies of the Victorian novel which have gone out of fashion in the twentieth century. They are moral edification, discussion of the characters with the reader, and an insistence on the ways in which actions illustrate human nature in general.

These three tendencies all bring the author to the reader's notice. They are the very things that Joyce, for example, wished to avoid. Stephen's well-known pronouncement towards the end of *The Portrait of the Artist as a Young Man* runs as follows:

> The artist, like the God of creation, remains within or behind or beyond or above his handiwork, refined out of existence, indifferent, paring his fingernails.

Beach issues a timely warning about our attitude to the Victorian method. We must be careful, he points out, not to assume that it is necessarily inferior. Naturally, we find the Victorian manner quaint. But we must not forget that we are 'dealing with masterpieces of fictional art perhaps greater than any that have since been produced'. It may even be that the disappearance of the author is—

> a kind of degeneration—accompanying the gradual decline in vigor and spontaneity. We are doubtless incapable of rightly appraising the art of our own day, an art which is expressive of our own state of mind. The best we can do is to make out what is the artistic principle involved in our preference for a different method of story-telling.   21-2

23

The increasing preoccupation of the nineteenth century with new methods of story-telling, with the well-constructed novel, stemmed largely from the French Naturalists—the Goncourts, Zola, Maupassant and Flaubert. The last-named was the key figure. With him the novelist became less an entertainer and more the high priest of an art-form. It was an attitude which became well known in England towards the end of the century, and which made Wilkie Collins's advice seem very innocent: 'Make 'em laugh, make 'em cry, make 'em wait.'

All this is of necessity a dangerous over-simplification. The Victorian novel was by no means purely an entertainment, an unselfconscious spinning of yarns. In a very interesting study (*The Theory of the Novel in England, 1850–70*), Richard Stang has shown that a great deal of very searching theorising about the novel went on, chiefly in such Victorian periodicals as the *Cornhill Magazine* and the *Westminster Review*. Novelists took themselves very seriously, and they and their critics had much to say of the novel's structure, of its morality and of its relationship to reality.

Nevertheless, a comparison between the aims of Wilkie Collins and Flaubert reveals the growing wish of novelists to be taken as seriously as poets. Ever since Aristotle, critics had thought of both verse and drama in relation to clearly formulated rules. Why should not the novel, even though a comparative newcomer to the literary scene, be accorded the same dignity? Was it not equally a form of art?

HENRY JAMES

In England it was above all Henry James who made these high claims for the novel. He theorised indefatigably. In 1884 he wrote two articles for *The Times Literary Supplement* entitled 'The Art of Fiction'. He later exchanged letters on the subject with Robert Louis Stevenson (another theorist), George Bernard Shaw, and H. G. Wells. And he wrote (a little sadly because he knew that people did not understand them) Prefaces to the New York edition of his novels.

James saw these Prefaces as the establishment of a working aesthetic for the novel. He wrote them, he told W. D. Howells, in a letter dated 17 August 1908, as 'a sort of plea for Criticism, for Discrimination, for Appreciation on other than infantile lines—as against the so almost universal Anglo-Saxon absence of these things'. The words doubtless reflect his own visits to Paris and indicate that his attitude could not easily recommend itself in England. H. G. Wells, for example, opposed it with typical assurance and vigour. He wrote an article entitled 'The Scope of the Novel', declaring that he wanted, like Shaw in the field of drama, to make it, and all art, serve the cause of improving the social order. James did not. He told Wells (*Henry James and H. G. Wells*, published by Hart-Davis, 1958):

> It is art that makes life, makes interest, makes importance. I know of no substitute whatever for the force and beauty of its possession. 267

Life itself was for James formless and meaningless. Art could give it form and meaning. It could do so only by selecting and arranging, not by wandering, Wellsian fashion, into territory that did not concern it. It is about this selecting and arranging that James theorised so much.

An indication of what art meant to him appears in the comment on Trollope at the start of his 1884 article. Trollope, he says, by admitting in his novels that he is only making believe, has betrayed his 'sacred office' and been guilty of a 'terrible crime'. They are solemn words and start us on the road which will end by substituting art for religion. A man 'making believe' cannot be 'occupied in looking for truth', and to James the novelist is so occupied, even more fully than the historian.

To examine James's theories in detail would be a long and complicated task. His insights were so delicate and so logically pursued that it is often difficult to follow them. R. P. Blackmur has said in his Introduction to the 'Critical Prefaces' (entitled *The Art of the Novel*) that James 'enjoyed an excess of intelligence and suffered, both in life and art, from an excessive effort to communicate it'. As a result, his theorising becomes superfine.

Wells's cruel picture of James in *Boon* is not surprising—his best-known sally describes the 'magnificent but painful hippopotamus' picking up a pea. But total rejection of James's insights is foolish. Anyone who wishes to understand what was happening in the novel at the end of the nineteenth century must attend to Henry James.

CONRAD AND FORD

At first glance, it seems unlikely that these considerations should have anything to do with Conrad. He was originally a sailor, not a literary man, and he knew no English until he was twenty-three. That he should have become a famous English novelist was extraordinary enough. Can we believe that he also concerned himself with literary theory?

That he did was partly the result of his facility in French. He must have known and shared Flaubert's uncompromising claims, as well as Maupassant's famous Preface to *Pierre et Jean* (1887), which became the artistic manifesto of the Realists. (It contains a section which carefully distinguishes the serious from the merely entertaining novel.) But it was even more the result of his association with Ford.

In 1898, when money was short and writing difficult, Conrad asked W. E. Henley to introduce him to a possible collaborator. Henley suggested Ford Madox Ford, then Ford Madox Hueffer. This last Pre-Raphaelite, as he has been called, enjoyed and took for granted that literary background which Conrad lacked and had to provide for himself. He had a flamboyant manner and spoke of art forms with easy assurance. Wells said that he was 'a great system of assumed personas and dramatised selves'.

The collaboration was not in itself significant. Its main result was a boys' adventure story, *Romance*. But it was accompanied by interminable discussions of literary theory just when Conrad was setting himself to learn the lessons of his art. They were a background to the writing of *Lord Jim* and *Nostromo*. Ford gave several accounts of them, and in *Joseph Conrad: A Personal*

Remembrance recorded some of their findings under the headings Impressionism, Selection, Structure, *Progression d'effet,* etc. Ford said that he himself—

> . . . probably knew more about words but Conrad certainly had an infinitely greater hold over the architectonics of the novel, over the way a story should be built up so that its interest progresses and grows up to the last word.   168-9

After Conrad's death, Ford left Europe for America where he established himself as a university lecturer and literary critic. With typical vigour and brashness he drew up a list of requirements for the serious novel. It appears in several of his books, but most clearly in *The English Novel* (1930). These requirements were most fully realised in the novels of James, Stephen Crane and Conrad, all of whom were, according to Ford, technical masters of their trade. Many of the great writers of the past, on the other hand—Defoe, Fielding, Sterne, Thackeray and Dickens—were only entertainers. They wrote 'nuvvles', which were little better than most escapist fiction, and they did so because their moral concerns were inadequate and the form of their works flawed by digressions.

It may be noted in passing that this position is very like that of F. R. Leavis in *The Great Tradition* (1948). Ford and Leavis both established standards by which to judge novels and then condemned whatever did not conform to their standards; both revered Jane Austen; both believed that the novel could, like any other art form, offer a special kind of truth.

There is no reason to suppose that Conrad would have accepted Ford's list of 'nuvvlists', though he would have understood the considerations underlying it. He would certainly have agreed with the insistence on the novel as an art form. It was an idea which found expression in the trend of the serious novels of the day, Conrad's among them. And Ford gave expression to an attitude towards the novel which came into its own with Henry James and is still with us over half a century later. A novel was art and art was an essential part of life. Ford likened

27

it to appreciation of the song the Syrens sang or of the Sermon on the Mount.

For such things alone can give you knowledge of the hearts, the necessities, the hopes and the fears of your fellow-men; and such knowledge alone can guide us through life without disaster.

THUS TO REVISIT, 7

3

The Impulse to Write

The mental processes of artistic creation are, and no doubt will remain, mysterious. With Conrad, whose life readily divides itself into two parts (the varied, active life at sea, and the unexciting literary life in England) they are particularly so. What impelled him to write at all? And why, in any case, in English?

Conrad's native tongue was Polish. His second language was French, learned when five at the hands of 'a good, ugly governess'. English he did not learn until, at the age of twenty-three, he joined the British Merchant Service.

It can never have been likely that he would write in Polish. Once exiled, he had few opportunities of using it; and as a sailor who later wrote much about the sea, he found it deficient in technical expressions. French, on the other hand, he was always fluent in. Its idiomatic expressions often appear in his work, notably in *Lord Jim* when the elderly French lieutenant is recalling how he boarded the 'Patt-na', and are also scattered interestingly throughout *A Personal Record*. Ford said that Conrad's more complicated sentences were translated direct from the French. Ford, it is true, is not a reliable biographer: he writes too much in his own praise, and when he does allow Conrad the centre of the stage, it is all too contrived and dramatised. Yet, unlikely though the above claim seems on the face of it, when Ford pictures Conrad and himself talking French, learning passages of Flaubert and Maupassant by heart, and translating them into English, the picture bears the stamp of truth. 'As the French say' is an expression common enough in Conrad to testify to his love of their language.

The fact remains that he wrote in English. It caused surprise early in his writing career. Before 1900, an article in the *North American Review* by Sir Hugh Clifford claimed that Conrad 'exercised a choice between the two languages French and English'. This 'misapprehension' Conrad is at pains to correct in the Author's Note to *A Personal Record*. Here is his disclaimer:

> The truth of the matter is that my faculty to write in English is as natural as any other aptitude with which I might have been born. I have a strange and overpowering feeling that it had always been an inherent part of myself. English was for me neither a matter of choice nor adoption. The merest idea of choice had never entered my head. And as to adoption—well, yes, there was adoption; but it was I who was adopted by the genius of the language, which directly I came out of the stammering stage made me its own so completely that its very idioms I truly believe had a direct action on my temperament and fashioned my still plastic character.   v

The action, he tells us, was 'very mysterious and for that reason too mysterious to explain'.

In coming to the language so late, Conrad knew two extremes of it—the direct, strong vigour of sailors' speech, and the literary language of his 'thick, green-covered volumes' of Shakespeare and of the Byron he bought while on leave from the 'Palestine'. At sea, he read whatever he could lay hands on. In *The Nigger of the Narcissus*, we find Singleton reading Bulwer Lytton. It may well stand as a picture of Conrad himself, who picked up novels by Mrs. Henry Wood and Miss Braddon as well as countless newspapers and magazines.

In correcting Sir Hugh Clifford, Conrad says that French is 'perfectly crystallised'. Ford puts the thought in this way:

> Conrad's indictment of the English language was this, that no English word is a word: that all English words are instruments for exciting blurred emotions. 'Oaken' in French means 'made

of oak wood'—nothing more. 'Oaken' in English connotes innumerable moral attributes: it will connote stolidity, resolution, honesty, blond features, relative unbreakableness, absolute unbendableness—also, made of oak. . . . The consequence is that no English word has clean edges . . .

JOSEPH CONRAD. A PERSONAL REMEMBRANCE, 214

Ford may be indicting the English language for himself rather than for Conrad. But there can be no doubt that it offered fitting expression for Conrad's complex vision of life. Writing of his early Malayan books to Edward Garnett, Conrad told him:

All is illusion . . . Every image floats vaguely in a sea of doubt —and the doubt itself is lost in an unexplored universe of incertitude.

F. R. Karl A READER'S GUIDE TO JOSEPH CONRAD, 33

Such a blurred vision needed blurred words, and this explains Conrad's assertion that it was the language which adopted him, not he the language.

THE CONCEPTION AND DEVELOPMENT OF 'ALMAYER'S FOLLY'

In section IV of *A Personal Record* Conrad gives a matter-of-fact account of how he wrote his first novel, *Almayer's Folly*. It shows his imagination using the raw material of his memory.

On the day he picked up his pen to start, he exhibited 'no signs of fine frenzy'; he was 'in no haste to take the plunge into his writing life, if as plunge this first attempt may be described'. In a mood of 'utter surrender to indolence', he was thinking of Almayer, perhaps because 'the opaline mist' at that moment shrouding his London lodgings in Bessborough Gardens was very like that around the wharf forty miles up a Bornean river where he had first seen the man two years before (*A Personal Record*, 69–73).

Conrad had heard a good deal of him before he met him. Often as he voyaged in the East, men had referred to Almayer and smiled—he was the odd fellow who kept geese and was the manager of a coal-mine, though it 'could not be worked because it was haunted by some particularly atrocious ghosts'. He was rarely successful and had ready explanations of the fact. Conrad saw him now because his ship had a pony for him, a pony which was duly swung on to the jetty where it escaped Almayer's control and ran off into the forest. Almayer was not put out. He conversed indirectly, avoiding plain answers and exuding a general air of grievance. He invited Conrad to dinner and Conrad found it impossible to refuse—'I accepted—and I am paying yet the price of my sanity. The possessor of the only flock of geese on the East Coast is responsible for the existence of some fourteen volumes, so far' (87).

Conrad states explicitly that when he started writing he had in his mind's eye an exact picture of Almayer—dressed in thin cotton singlet and wide blue and yellow trousers, a curly wisp of black hair straying across his forehead (74–5). This was his starting-point. William Faulkner confessed to having a similar one:

> With me a story usually begins with a single idea or memory or mental picture. The writing of the story is simply a matter of working up to that moment, to explain why it happened or what it caused to follow.
>
> WRITERS AT WORK ed. Cowley, 132

Conrad said much the same thing:

> . . . [I write] toward some fixed event or scene I can see.
>
> Gordan, 103

So vivid were these scenes that he often drew pictures and diagrams of them in his manuscripts; so determined was he to dramatise them that he would sometimes interrupt his writing to enact an incident, either alone or with the help of his wife.

Proust used such moments of recollection to sustain an elaborate theory of memory and time. He patterns *A la recherche du temps perdu* with images (the vases are a good example) which evoke the fragrance of the past; he continually links moments widely separated in time; and in a famous passage in the first volume he analyses the way in which in later life, the taste of a biscuit ('*la petite madeleine*') which his aunt used to give him when he was a very small child, recalls in detail for him that life of long ago. Out of such memories Proust fashioned an entire artistic world—just as paper, made into crumbs and steeped in water, Japanese fashion, 'stretches and bends, takes on colour and distinctive shape, becomes flowers or houses or people, permanent and recognisable'. So it was with Conrad and his visual memory. His novels grew out of it.

How, then, was a novel built around a remembered scene? In the case of Almayer, the building began two years after the first vivid meeting with him, and continued a further four years. Conrad tells us what his mind was doing with Almayer in that time. He often thought of him—his own expression is that Almayer 'haunted' him. He thought of him as a man who failed, a man who came to him first on men's lips 'stripped of all prestige by men's queer smiles and the disrespectful chatter of every vagrant trader in the Islands. Your name was the common property of the winds; it, as it were, floated naked over the waters about the equator.' It was this conception of Almayer that he united to his picture of him when he started to write. Conrad claimed that he—

> wrapped round Almayer's form the royal mantle of the tropics and essayed to put into the hollow sound the very anguish of paternity.
>
> A PERSONAL RECORD, 88

If, in the Elysian fields, Almayer complains that the picture is an unkind misrepresentation, 'one not worthy of his merits', Conrad will have only one reply:

> I believed in you in the only way it was possible for me to believe . . . You were always an unlucky man, Almayer. Nothing was ever quite worthy of you. What made you so real to me was that you held this lofty theory with some force of conviction and with admirable consistency. 88

Here, then, was Conrad's main interest in Almayer—he was a man who failed but believed unshakably that life had failed him. And if Almayer 'haunted' Conrad after the first meeting, Conrad must have spent many hours with his ghost. It gave him a theme that remained with him to the end. It stems, on the evidence of his picture of Heyst's father in *Victory* and of our knowledge of Conrad's youth, from memories of Korzeniowski, aristocrat and talented pursuer of ideals, exiled, broken and dying in Warsaw. When Conrad thought of the great silent demonstration that was his father's funeral, it seemed to him a testimony not so much to the man as to his unfailing loyalty to a doomed idea, the idea of a free Poland.

Conrad extended this idea of failure in a way which had nothing to do with his father. He was four and a half years writing *Almayer's Folly*, and the manuscript accompanied him on a visit to his uncle in Russia and up the Congo to the Stanley Falls. During this time, Conrad said, the book 'was never dismissed from his mind even when the hope of finishing it was very faint' (*A Personal Record*, 68). It is basically about a man who fails himself, who betrays his own integrity. For Almayer is the first of Conrad's heroes whose lives are based on a lie. He has allowed a much older man, Tom Lingard, to make important decisions for him, instead of making his own way in the world. Deceived by the glitter of Lingard's potential fortune (Conrad tells us that he was 'gifted with a strong and active imagination and saw, as in a flash of dazzling light, great piles of shining guilders' [10]), he accepts the inheritance on condition that he marries Lingard's adopted black daughter. From this initial mistake spring all his later woes, culminating in his desertion by his own daughter, Nina.

Inspired in the first place by the strong visual memory of Almayer and his world, Conrad builds his story around the idea of self-betrayal. *Almayer's Folly* is the first of many novels dealing with moral failure.

HOW 'THE SECRET AGENT' CAME TO BE WRITTEN
Conrad gave an equally revealing account of the genesis of *The Secret Agent* over ten years later. The novel (which is

examined on pp. 125-32) appeared in 1907, but the Author's Note telling of its origin was not written until 1920. It shows that it was conceived very much like *Almayer's Folly*, and offers another glimpse into the mysteries of artistic creation.

It tells how Conrad was discussing casually with Ford the folly of anarchy. 'Presently, passing to particular instances, we recalled the already old story of the attempt to blow up the Greenwich Observatory' (x). Conrad remarked that the outrage 'could not be laid hold of mentally in any sort of way' (x), which presumably meant that it was impossible to ascribe any motive or meaning to so senseless a piece of violence. But Ford explained the incident with the words: 'Oh, that fellow was half an idiot. His sister committed suicide afterwards.' This gave Conrad his first clear hint of the novel to come. The 'illuminating quality' of those words was such that he felt like one 'walking out of a forest on to a plain'. For a time he contemplated the words and incident 'in a passive way'.

About a week later, happening to read the recollections of a Police Officer, Conrad was suddenly struck by a few perfectly ordinary lines of dialogue. In particular, this angry sally arrested him:

> All that's very well. But your idea of secrecy over there seems to consist of keeping the Home Secretary in the dark.   xi

Conrad admits that there is nothing memorable in these words. Still, there must have been—

> some sort of atmosphere in the whole incident because all of a sudden I felt myself stimulated. And then ensued in my mind what a student of chemistry would best understand from the analogy of the addition of the tiniest little drop of the right kind, precipitating the process of crystallisation in a test tube containing some colourless solution.   xi

Then follow two crucial paragraphs, explaining what happened between that point and the writing of the novel. The first one describes the visual activity of the mind, the second the gradual adoption of a unifying idea. It seems best to quote them in full.

> It was at first for me a mental change, disturbing a quieted-down imagination, in which strange forms, sharp in outline but imperfectly apprehended, appeared and claimed attention as crystals will do by their bizarre and unexpected shapes. One fell to musing before the phenomenon—even of the past: of South America, a continent of crude sunshine and brutal revolutions, of the sea, the vast expanse of salt waters, the mirror of heaven's frowns and smiles, the reflector of the world's light. Then the vision of an enormous town presented itself, of a monstrous town more populous than some continents and in its man-made might as if indifferent to heaven's frowns and smiles; a cruel devourer of the world's light. There was room enough there to place any story, depth enough for any passion, variety enough for any setting, darkness enough to bury five millions of lives.
>
> Irresistibly the town became the background for the ensuing period of deep and tentative meditations. Endless vistas opened before me in various directions. It would take years to find the right way! It seemed to take years! . . . Slowly the dawning conviction of Mrs. Verloc's maternal passion grew up to a flame between me and that background, tingeing it with its secret ardour and receiving from it in exchange some of its own sombre colouring. At last the story of Winnie Verloc stood out complete from the days of her childhood to the end, unproportioned as yet, with everything still on the first plan, as it were; but ready now to be dealt with. It was a matter of about three days.   xi–xii

The interesting thing here is the distance we have come from Conrad's starting point. There were two initial impressions, the explosion and the half idiot whose sister committed suicide. Conrad tried to imagine a background for them. At first he pictured a vast, violent and hostile continent. Then his reading of the Police Officer's reminiscences suggested the teeming city, dark and indifferent. Unlike the continent, it was man-made; its layers of society were bound together in one gloomy meaninglessness. Conrad would bury his story in that. From what point of view, towards what end? This was the point at which

Conrad conceived not another picture, but an idea—that of an obsessed woman. The great city would form the backcloth, but in the foreground would be the personal tragedy of the Verloc family. Once he had reached that point, the rest was technique, what he called 'the proportion' of the whole.

4

From Dilettante to Serious Novelist

Conrad once said that his second novel was prompted by
Garnett's suggestion, 'Why not write another?'. This was not
true. Conrad had started *An Outcast of the Islands* before he
met Garnett. He still had no thought of becoming a professional
writer, but expected to return to sea. Once again, he chose the
Malayan setting. Some of the characters are the same, too,
though the events take place before those in *Almayer's Folly*.

'AN OUTCAST OF THE ISLANDS'
The first sentence of *An Outcast* shows that its main theme is
unchanged.

> When he stepped off the straight and narrow path of his peculiar
> honesty, it was with an inward assertion of unflinching resolve
> to fall back again into the monotonous but safe stride of virtue
> as soon as his little excursion into the wayside quagmires had
> produced the desired effect.

Typically, it is an image; honesty is a straight, narrow path,
dishonesty an excursion into a quagmire. It suggests at once
that honesty is the usual and desirable state of man, for monotonous and safe though it is, it is contrasted with the 'little
excursion' of dishonesty. There is irony in the meaning and
sound of the words 'desired effect'. They point to the moral
danger of an action whose effects not even the most 'unflinching
resolve' will be able to control. The sentence, in short, anticipates
the later novels.

The story imitates that of *Almayer's Folly*: Peter Willems, the hero, has been entrusted by Lingard with the secret of the channel which gives access to his highly successful trading post. He is also passionately in love with a native girl, Aissa. During Lingard's absence, she allows Willems to marry her in return for his revelation to the Malayans of the means of navigating the channel. After this, the Malay chiefs have no further use for him and refuse to accept him into their society. Lingard is equally adamant, when he at last returns. Willems pleads with him to be taken away so that he can make yet another start somewhere else, but Lingard orders him to stay where he is. While attempting to escape, Willems is killed by Aissa.

Conrad's second novel, then, repeats (at much greater length) his first. The themes are still betrayal, the dangers of imagining a splendid future, the tensions between black and white, the perils of isolation. They remained obsessions throughout his writing career, because his attitude to life was mature before he became a novelist. He knew what he had to say; his problem was how to say it.

Both *Almayer's Folly* and *An Outcast* suffer from inadequate technique. Their stories move slowly and unevenly, their characters are neither fully realised nor sufficiently differentiated, and their prose is too consciously literary. A typical sentence from *Almayer* begins:

> As he skirted in his weary march the edge of the forest he glanced now and then into its dark shade, so enticing in its deceptive appearance of coolness, so repellent with its unrelieved gloom, where lay, entombed and rotting . . .   166–7

The adjectives here insist too protestingly, and the highly artificial rhythm strains too much. H. G. Wells made a shrewd comment in reviewing *An Outcast*:

> Mr. Conrad is wordy . . . He has still to learn the great half of his art, the art of leaving things unwritten.
>
> Baines, 165–6

Conrad admitted in *A Personal Record* that *Almayer's Folly* was begun in idleness as a holiday task, and the fact is that neither it nor its successor was written to a clear plan. This has been proved beyond doubt by J. D. Gordan in *Joseph Conrad. The Making of a Novelist*. The fourth chapter of this fascinating book compares the different versions of Conrad's texts and reaches this conclusion:

> The study of Conrad's habits of composition substantiates his claim that he wrote first and theorised later . . . He felt his way towards the plot of his stories and towards the best presentation of his material. 173

Gordan shows that this was true as late as *Lord Jim* (1900). As we have seen, it was through association with Ford that Conrad learned to plan his novels as more conscious wholes and thus took his place alongside Henry James as an architect of novels, but it was a slow process. For a long time his development of his plots retained hazardous features. (There are some good comments on this in chapters IV and V of F. R. Karl's *A Reader's Guide to Joseph Conrad*.)

It was the same, Gordan shows, with *The Rescue*, another Malayan novel which Conrad began after *An Outcast*. He tried a number of plans, destroyed countless pages and finally brought himself to a standstill. This time paralysis of the power to write left him desperate. It is significant that when he resumed it in 1916, he cut it by almost half. Part of the original trouble was very likely that Conrad was persisting in overworking his first inspiration, Malaya. He lacked a new setting and an adequate technique.

He took an important step towards finding both when he interrupted work on *The Rescue* to start *The Nigger of the Narcissus* (1897). It is his first undisputed masterpiece.

'THE NIGGER OF THE NARCISSUS'

The issues of this tale all meet in James Wait, the nigger. From the moment he attracts attention by being almost late for the roll-call, the life of the whole ship revolves round him. It is his baleful presence that starts Belfast thieving, that exaggerates the cook's near-religious mania, and that allows the despicable

Donkin to achieve a position as the mouthpiece of the crew. Without the nigger, we are given to understand, Mr. Baker, the mate, would have had no difficulty in dealing with Donkin, who at first gets little sympathy from his shipmates. With Wait, however, Mr. Baker is powerless—'nonplussed by a unique experience'. Whether the nigger is actually dying or merely malingering, the crew cannot decide. Old Singleton is the one man untouched by Wait's presence (41–4).

The men are ultimately saved by a great storm, saved, that is, in the sense that they again pull together in their effort to defeat their common enemy, the sea. Here the story touches sublimity without becoming ponderous or wordy. At the height of the tempest Mr. Baker asks the cook to make a hot drink. The cook is at first too busy talking about the life to come. Mr. Baker says he will attempt the job himself, but the cook is not having that. He begins to scramble towards the shambles that is his kitchen, shouting into the teeth of the gale: 'Galley . . . my business . . . As long as she swims I will cook.' The saying becomes a byword (and is Conrad's affirmation of that devotion to the task in hand which, he implies, is the best way of living). The cook finds his stove 'reared up on end' and is forced, the crew surmise, 'to use his breadboard for a raft'. Even so, at the risk of his life, he achieves the apparently impossible and puts fresh heart into the weary men (81–4). As old Singleton has said at the start of the voyage when asked what kind of ship this was: 'Ships are all right. It's the men in them' (24). And the men in this one, after burying James Wait at sea, reach home in a 'Narcissus' which runs quickly on 'as if relieved of an unfair burden'.

The story thus briefly summarised is in the first place a well-told yarn. There are, it is true, one or two lapses into the wordiness of the two Malayan novels already published—the paragraphs describing the progress of the 'Narcissus' after entering 'the chops of the channel' are the most obvious example (161). But the blemishes are few and unimportant. In *The Nigger*, Conrad has for the first time successfully mastered the technique of his new calling.

The Nigger is more than a yarn of the sea. Conrad leaves us in no doubt that his ship is the greater world in miniature:

> The sun looked upon her all day, and every morning rose with a burning, round stare of undying curiosity. She had her own future; she was alive with the lives of those who trod her decks; like the earth which had given her up to the sea, she had an intolerable load of regrets and hopes. On her lived timid truth and audacious lies; and, like the earth, she was unconscious, fair to see—and condemned by men to an ignoble fate.   29–30

Conrad's concern is with the health of the whole crew in the face of forces which threaten to poison their combined action.

The important thing is that the story is left to speak for itself. The details of seamanship are succinctly described, and the characters, modelled on the men with whom Conrad had sailed in earlier days, are set before us with the same sparing yet clear touches (like the cook, with his religious mania, or the brisk and authoritative Mr. Baker). There are some splendid surprises which are not spoiled by authorial comment. One of the best is the signing off of the 'venerable' Singleton. At sea, his hands never hesitated; now he can hardly find the small pile of gold in the profound darkness of the shore. 'Can't write?' said the clerk, shocked. 'Make a mark, then.' With difficulty, Singleton does so. 'What a disgusting old brute', says the clerk, as the 'patriarchal seaman' passes out of sight, 'without as much as a glance' at anyone. Yet he has been 'the ship's completed wisdom', the man who, if anyone, has in his few words dropped the clearest hints about the implication and interpretation of events. It is Singleton's occasional dry comments that are signposts to make certain that the reader cannot miss the issues under consideration. Yet he is illiterate. (There is a comment on this on p. 113.)

The short scene of James Wait's burial at sea is a good indication of the measure of Conrad's newly found technical mastery (157–61). Surprisingly, it is Belfast who helps the sailmaker to prepare Jimmy for final surrender to the sea. He arranges two holystones, now this way, now that. Conrad has him doing this to the accompaniment of the sailmaker's plying needle and furious smoking. As, without delay, the tale moves into the moment of the reading of the burial service, its rhythm slows down and the crew are shown standing still, either embarrassed or uncomprehending. The words 'To the deep' are pronounced. At this point Conrad produces a very brief but weird and highly dramatic episode. The body will not move. 'Higher! Lift!' people whisper angrily. Belfast emits a passionate shriek—'Jimmy, be a man!' 'Go', he shouts again and again. He actually touches the dead man's head, whereupon 'the grey package' moves towards its ocean grave. This is not only exciting; it is also a final comment on the central mystery of the story—what is the secret of James Wait's inexplicable hold on everyone? Will it be exercised even after his death? 'Amen', Mr. Baker can at last say. 'Square the yards', thunders a voice. It is typical of Conrad to use such a sailing technicality to jolt his reader back to the ordinary routine of living. A breeze is coming. Like water in *The Waste Land*, it represents spiritual health. 'What did I tell you?' old Singleton mutters. 'I knowed it—he's gone and here it comes.' Without James Wait, the disciplined ship's community can once again act purposefully, 'wringing out meaning' together.

Perhaps the most important result of *The Nigger* was that its subject—the undermining of the spiritual health of a ship's crew—gave Conrad for the first time a clearly defined and limited theme. The main cause of his abandonment of *The Rescue* was very likely that in this case he did not know what he wanted to say. In turning from Malaya to his own experience at sea, he found himself as a novelist.

5

The Role of the Artist

Conrad recognised the importance of the change represented
by *The Nigger of the Narcissus* since, soon after finishing it, he
provided it with a Preface by way of a confession of faith. He
set himself, he tells, 'almost without laying down his pen' to
writing the Preface 'to express the spirit in which he was entering
on the task of his new life'. It shows that he was aware of more
than simple development from dilettantism to severe profes-
sionalism. With the conscious and austere dedication which we
associate with Henry James or James Joyce, he chose the high
calling of art.

THE PREFACE TO 'THE NIGGER'
The Preface is quite short and seems easy to follow. Yet it has
its own indirections which result from the oblique approach
typical of the Conrad who told his tales through Marlow and
who so often broke the natural time sequence. What follows is
an attempt at a logical and simplified summary (vii–xii).

People readily accept, Conrad argues, the importance of
thinkers and scientists. These are professional men who work
hard to present us with truths about the world we live in. The
thinker deals in ideas, the scientist in facts. Both help us in 'the
hazardous business of living'.

The artist is just as much a professional man. But whereas
thinkers and scientists look outside themselves for their material,
artists look within themselves. In so doing, they appeal to the
inner selves of their audience. As a result the work of artists
makes its appeal quietly and without fuss. Yet it is not the less

powerful on that account. Successive generations query the theories of thinkers and debate the facts of scientists; they accept with delight fine works of art. This is because art speaks to 'our capacity for delight and wonder, to the sense of mystery surrounding our lives; to our sense of pity, and beauty, and pain, to the latent feeling of fellowship with all creation . . .' (viii). Nor is there any place or character too obscure to be capable of revealing these values.

Conrad now states, rather oddly as though he is making a specially important point, that his 'avowal is not yet complete'. He wishes to make it plain that fiction appeals to 'temperament', and that it does so by using written words to move readers emotionally. Words, Conrad notes, are difficult things. They have been 'defaced by careless usage'. This has made it hard for the novelist to find the precise combination of them which will call up accurately for the reader's eye and ear the statement or view of the world which he wishes to present. The novelist who is an artist is not setting out to keep his readers amused or to teach them a lesson—he is catching and recording the complex pattern of life as he sees it.

He is, before all, making his reader *see* (the italics are Conrad's own); he is aspiring to 'the plasticity of sculpture, to the colour of painting, and to the magic suggestiveness of music'. In reaching this point in the Preface, Conrad has expanded and justified its second sentence: 'Art itself may be defined as a single-minded attempt to render the highest kind of justice to the visible universe, by bringing to light the truth, manifold and one, underlying its every aspect.'

For a second time in the Preface Conrad now insists that he has more to say. This catching in a mirror of the passing moment is, he stresses, 'only the beginning of the task'. For the resultant word-picture will, at its most successful, do two things: it will reveal the substance of the moment's truth and it will awaken in the heart of the reader a sense of solidarity with other men. To put it another way, it will, by presenting fleeting moments of life, explore the meaning of the human situation.

To look at novel-writing like this is to set aside as irrelevant such labels as 'realism', 'romanticism' or 'naturalism'. They are merely 'temporary formulas' and will not take a writer very far.

> But when he does succeed—behold!—all the truth of life is there: a moment of vision, a sigh, a smile—and the return to an eternal rest.   xii

As though recognising that all this theory is worth little compared with practice, Conrad has recourse to an image which will communicate meaning. Here it is in full:

> Sometimes, stretched at ease in the shade of a roadside tree, we watch the motions of a labourer in a distant field, and after a time, begin to wonder languidly as to what the fellow may be at. We watch the movements of his body, the wavings of his arms, we see him bend down, stand up, hesitate, begin again. It may add to the charm of an idle hour to be told the purpose of his exertions. If we know he is trying to lift a stone, to dig a ditch, to uproot a stump, we look with a more real interest at his efforts; we are disposed to condone the jar of his agitation upon the restfulness of the landscape; and even, if in a brotherly frame of mind, we may bring ourselves to forgive his failure. We understood his object, and, after all, the fellow has tried, and perhaps he had not the strength—and perhaps he had not the knowledge. We forgive, go on our way—and forget. And so it is with the workman of art.   xi

The Preface is Conrad's most explicit general statement about the art of the novelist. Usually, he avoided theorising about his work, and once wrote (in his Preface to 'The Shorter Tales', now most easily accessible in *Last Essays*) that an author's feelings towards his own creation were so deep and complex that the disclosing of them was dangerous. This may well explain why so many of his Prefaces are disappointing; they deal with what seem trivialities, and deal with them in a cursory, unplanned kind of way. Perhaps it explains, too, his strangely reticent and misleading subtitles—*Nostromo* is 'A tale of the sea-board', and *The Secret Agent* (of all things!) 'A simple tale'. But on this one occasion of the writing of *The Nigger*, fired no doubt by the excitement of choosing for career the practice of an art form, Conrad formulated some general considerations about it.

James Joyce's similar formulations of aesthetic theory in the *Portrait of the Artist as a Young Man*, are part of Stephen's growing-up, part of the story itself. In the earlier version, *Stephen Hero*, there is one idea which does not appear in the *Portrait* and which has an obvious affinity to Conrad's assertions. It is the announcement of the theory of 'epiphanies' (the showing-forth). Stephen looks at the clock of the Ballast Office and says that even that is capable of an epiphany—and by epiphany he means 'a sudden spiritual manifestation'. Artists, Stephen says, must record them with extreme care as they are 'delicate and evanescent moments'—an epiphany is like the groping of a spiritual eye until the vision is adjusted to exact focus. It is an idea very like 'the rescued fragments' of life which the artist is called on to 'snatch in a moment of courage', in the Preface to *The Nigger*.

There are scattered references to theories of art in Conrad's letters, and in an essay entitled 'Books' (in *Notes on Life and Letters*) he repeats some of the ideas of the Preface to *The Nigger*. The writing of fiction is, he claims, extremely difficult. Prompted by 'the flight of imaginative thought', it should rise above both classifications and artistic arrogance. (There is also one piece of typical advice to novelists to 'mature the strength of their imagination amongst the things of this earth'.) But Conrad was a practitioner rather than a theoretician. In the world of art, it is the individual work of art that counts. The generalisations of the Preface are certainly interesting, particularly in that with them Conrad marks the end of his tutelage in the novel. But the most significant achievement, pointing the way to the greatness to come, is *The Nigger of the Narcissus* itself. Years after its publication, he wrote in the copy which he gave his friend, Richard Curle, 'By these pages I stand or fall' (Gordan, 236). It is a fearless declaration.

THE STRUGGLE TO WRITE

In committing himself, however, to the role of artist, he was to make his life very hard. For usually he wrote only with the greatest difficulty. This is not altogether surprising. His lack of money, lavish spending, indifferent health and disorganised method of working did not make for the frame of mind which enabled Trollope to write two hundred and fifty words a page and at least twenty pages a week, year in, year out. Conrad's various publishers soon learned to expect material late, or the short story to grow without warning into the long novel, or the copy to stop altogether. What is surprising is the extreme desperation of his difficulty. He never outgrew it. There were times with *Almayer's Folly* when he was too drained of ideas and words to go on; and as late as 1920 he told a friend that he could 'get no prose of any kind out of himself' (Baines, 422). His worst agonies were experienced in mid-career over *Lord Jim* and *Nostromo*, at a time when he was recognised to be an important novelist but not financially successful. His letters of this time refer continually and in almost hysterical terms to his incapacity to write. He gives an impression in section V of *A Personal Record* of 'the strain of creative effort', and suggests a material parallel in 'the everlasting sombre stress of the Westward Winter passage round Cape Horn' (99).

Why was this? There is no evidence that Conrad felt similarly about his ordinary duties as a sailor. Ford, it is true, claimed that Conrad 'hated the sea', but this does not seem to mean more than that he lamented his small stature, found repetitive tasks monotonous, and was distrustful of the sea's terrible power; and against these misgivings we must put his frequently confessed love of the sea. But in any case, not even the theatrical Ford's suggestion of hatred comes near the exaggerated despair of Conrad's attitude to writing. However often the perfectionist in him may have made him consign page after page to the wastepaper basket, there remains something mysterious about his repeated confessions of total inability to create. Not even Flaubert, declaiming his sentences to the air on the terrace, tortured himself as Conrad did.

No doubt there was something of a pose in it. The romantic idea of the artist as a tortured soul was common enough by the end of the century. Particularly in France, artists were keenly aware of their separation from society. Baudelaire, with his deliberate adoption of a personality different from that of the ordinary man, is an obvious example. Obsessed by his isolation and unhappiness, he consciously cultivated the mystique of the artist. He likened the poet to an albatross, regal among the clouds but so ridiculously clumsy on earth as to be for ordinary men a mere object of mockery. Flaubert shared this view. And Conrad was certainly aware of it, as is indicated by a letter that he wrote in 1905 to Edmund Gosse, thanking him for his part in an award of £500 for services to literature. Here is part of it:

> I had just emerged from such a period of utter mistrust when Rothenstein's letter came to hand revealing to me the whole extent of your belief and the length to which you have taken the trouble to prove it—even to the length of making another mind share in your conviction. I accept this revelation with eagerness. I need not tell you that this moral support of belief is the greatest help a writer can receive in those difficult moments which Baudelaire has defined happily as 'les stérilités des écrivains nerveux'. Quincey too, I believe, has known that anguished suspension of all power of thought that comes to one often in the midst of a very revel of production, like the slave with his *memento mori* at a feast.
>
> JOSEPH CONRAD: LIFE AND LETTERS II, 14

Or perhaps the explanation of Conrad's difficulty in writing is simpler; perhaps he lacked the ability to organise his life. On board ship, routine was imposed on him; as a writer he had to make his own discipline. How was he to start, and having started, to continue? He made some revealing comments along these lines to Garnett, as he slowly ground to a halt with his first attempt at *The Rescue*:

> I am frightened when I remember that I have to drag it all out of myself. Other writers have some starting point. Something to catch hold of. They start from an anecdote . . . while I don't. I have had some impressions, some sensations—in my time— impressions and sensations of common things. And it's all faded.
>
> JOSEPH CONRAD: LIFE AND LETTERS I, 192

Baines, his biographer, comments that this was a state of mind; that the varied life of Conrad would have been the envy of any other novelist, who would have found in it ample material for countless novels. He adds: 'but it may be that he was feeling the effect of his nomadic life, of being an expatriate and thus unable to draw on a body of experience common to his prospective readers' (174).

This may be so. But it is difficult to avoid thinking that there was a deeper reason for his difficulties. Conrad noted in the familiar Preface to *A Personal Record* that one of the main reasons for his 'special piety' towards the sea life of his past, was that it made demands to which youth and strength could respond; its disciplines prevented 'a young conscience' from being perplexed (xiv).

In the realm of art there are no such obvious disciplines. A novelist, Conrad notes, seeks his material in the 'interior world' of his thoughts and emotions, where 'there are no policemen, no law, no pressure of circumstances or dread of opinion to keep him within bounds'. Who then, he asks, 'is going to say Nay to his temptations if not his conscience?' (xviii).

Conrad is here speaking of a theme which bulks large in his novels—the power of man's deeper instincts and desires to destroy his self-control. In the early work, the conflict between the two is often represented by the clash of white and black (Almayer's ability to control his destiny is undermined by his marriage to a Malay woman; Willems's downfall, in *An Outcast of the Islands*, is accelerated by the passionate sensuality of his love for Aissa; and Marlow himself, for all his rationalising, is almost conquered by the African heart of darkness). Later, the treatment of the war in man between reason and decency on the one hand, and his dark hidden reaches on the other, takes different form (see p. 108). But continually, Conrad is aware and fearful of the hidden, mysterious places in men's minds.

Once again, it has to be admitted that there may be in this a certain posturing. Many nineteenth-century poets, English, German and French, saw and wrote of the artist as a Satanic figure, licensed to practise the unlawful. Baudelaire openly pronounced himself a Satanist. But Conrad, though perhaps influenced by the intellectual climate that produced Baudelaire's attitude, could never (as we have seen at the start of this section) contain his creation within the bounds of any kind of 'ism'. He compared the power to produce great imaginative literature to the holding of a magic wand, adding:

> to be a great magician one must surrender oneself to occult and irresponsible powers.
>
> A PERSONAL RECORD xvii

'Surrender' is the alarming word here. To surrender to the call of the sea was permissible and safe—the age-old traditions of the service kept one safe; to surrender to art was risky—only a 'regard for decency' could prevent one from indulging in the debased coinage of insincere emotion or of unlawful obsessions.

> It may be my sea-training acting upon a natural disposition to keep good hold on the one thing really mine, but the fact is that I have a positive horror of losing even for one moment that full possession of myself which is the first condition of good service. And I have carried my notion of good service from my earlier into my later existence.
>
> A PERSONAL RECORD xvii

There are other hints in Conrad's writings which suggest that he both feared and was fascinated by his own imagination. He knew that an artist's 'enigmatic side' was obscure 'even to himself', and described it as 'an unconscious response to the past from which his work is derived'. To this unconscious response he adopted a guarded attitude. Dostoevsky did not, and Conrad characterised him as a 'grimacing, haunted creature' who produced 'fierce mouthings from prehistoric ages' (*Joseph Conrad: Life and Letters* II, 192 and 140). It has often been suggested that the indignation with which Conrad always rejected any comments on his Russian and tormented soul, reveals a deep fear that the comment might be true. Perhaps, in other words, he was like the grimacing and haunted Dostoevsky to whom he was so hostile. If so, we can the more easily understand that he would have a divided attitude towards the act of writing. If the realm of art both attracted and repelled him, the fact goes a long way to explaining the terrible wrestlings he underwent to produce so many of his novels. It explains why the word 'conscience' appears so often in *A Personal Record*, and why Conrad claimed that if an artist was to bear 'true testimony' to his view of the world, 'nothing except conscience' could guide him (92).

6

Technique 1:
Story and Character

Conrad's main achievements extend from 1897 to 1915. During these years he experimented continually. I shall consider this experimentation before tracing the development of his thought.

The simplest way of understanding why Conrad experimented is to try writing a novel. Since everyone imagines people and places at one time or another, it ought not to be difficult. All that is necessary is to give a straightforward account of a number of events in the order in which they occur. It turns out to be by no means as easy as it sounds.

For one thing, the places where events happen need describing. Unless the scene is realised at enormous length, this will involve the selection of a few significant details. Then the events themselves will not be of equal importance, and the novelist will have to decide which to tell in detail and which to pass quickly over. Again, the characters involved in the story not only act but have thoughts and feelings. How are these to be described? And, since not all the characters can be brought before the reader at the same moment, although they are doing things simultaneously, what is to happen to the straightforward time-scheme which seems at first sight the obvious one? These awkward questions could be multiplied.

It is obvious that each novelist will have his own way of going about his task. Some are likely to be fairly straightforward, and some much less so. The briefest acquaintance with Conrad's longer works will tell us that his approach to story-telling was very complicated, more complicated than that of, say, Jane Austen. A closer comparison may make this plain.

Jane Austen starts *Emma* by introducing her main characters with firm judgments—Emma herself, 'handsome, clever, and rich, with a comfortable home and happy disposition', has had 'rather too much of her own way'; her one-time governess is marrying Mr. Weston, 'a man of unexceptionable character, easy fortune and pleasant manners'; Mr. Knightley is 'sensible' and 'an old and intimate friend'. And having started so clearly, this great novel continues in the same way. Everything that happens is seen from Emma's point of view, through her eyes.

The opening of *Victory* is very different, though it is one of Conrad's more straightforward novels and, like *Emma*, is unified round one central figure. The reader gathers that Axel Heyst is the hero, but has no clear impression of his character. Heyst, in fact, has a large number of contradictory nicknames— 'Enchanted', 'Hard Facts', 'Utopist' Heyst, among many others (7–8). His job and past history are equally baffling. Having learned on the first page that 'The Tropical Belt Coal Company went into liquidation', the reader follows Heyst's career before he became that firm's tropical manager; and then learns from the report of a man named Davidson (who, in turn, has got much of his information from a hotel-keeper, Schomberg) that Heyst has run off with a young English girl. At this point Conrad again steps back in time and recounts the events which led up to Heyst's flight with the girl—and this indirection is nothing compared with the tortuous development of *Chance*.

How can we explain the difference between Jane Austen's and Conrad's methods? There is no easy answer. Jane Austen, like her readers, saw the world of her day very clearly—that is to say, she knew precisely what values she wished her novel to mirror. Conrad found the world much less clear. Heyst's many nicknames are all aspects of his character as other people see him, and who is to say which is the truest one? Conrad's obliqueness is not a method specially assumed for writing a different kind of novel. It results naturally from his way of looking at life, from his wish to mirror the complexity of human beings. In Conrad, as in all serious art, technique and theme are intricately bound together.

To consider the novels critically will involve separating aspects of technique and theme. We must look, for example, at Conrad's time shifts, his use of a narrator, and the kinds of men and women that interest him; and we may perhaps hope that after this critical examination we shall understand the novels better. But we must not make the mistake of supposing that reading about works of art is a substitute for the works themselves. The most that reading about literary art forms can do is to send us back to the original texts in the hope that we shall more fully appreciate them. All this breaking down into individual aspects is highly artificial; not to understand this leads to serious distortions and misunderstandings. So before taking the risk, let us consider a warning from Henry James in *The Art of Fiction*:

> People often talk of these things as if they had a kind of internecine distinctness, instead of melting into each other at every breath, and being intimately associated parts of one general effort of expression. I cannot imagine composition existing in a series of blocks, nor conceive, in any novel worth discussing at all, of a passage of description that is not in its intention narrative, a passage of dialogue that is not in its intention descriptive, a touch of truth of any sort that does not partake of the nature of incident, or an incident that derives its interest from any other source than the general and only source of the success of a work of art—that of being illustrative. A novel is a living thing, all one and continuous, like any other organism, and in proportion as it lives will it be found, I think, that in each of the parts there is something of each of the other parts.
>
> 12–13

ROMANTIC GLAMOUR

Novels are in the first place stories. 'Oh dear, yes', said E. M. Forster, 'I were it was not so'. But the protest does not alter the fact. Novels describe people acting.

The most obvious feature of Conrad's stories is that they are melodramatic. He is the novelist of extreme situation. His heroes may be in total isolation, or driven to suicide, or faced with the choice between betraying a friend or ruining their own careers—all situations from his best-known works.

The evidence of the short stories, which revolve more clearly round one basic idea, is just as clear. A Russian soldier has to discharge a debt of honour by killing his erstwhile helper (*The Warrior's Soul*), or a man is first unjustly sentenced, then pardoned by the government, then leads a rebellion against it (*Gaspar Ruiz*).

These events are often acted out in exotic lands and against climates of tropical violence. Storms accompany the climaxes of *Victory* and *The Rover*, and inky blackness heightens the ordeal of Nostromo and Decoud on the Golfo Placido. Theatrical exaggeration seems to be one of Conrad's hallmarks.

All this suggests that Conrad is a romantic writer in the sense that he is concerned with the highly coloured, the implausible, the mysterious—that he is a writer who, in Hawthorne's words (in the Preface to *The House of the Seven Gables*), 'swerves aside from the truth of the human heart' instead of aiming at 'a very minute fidelity to the probable and ordinary course of man's experience'. If so, his place in the history of the English novel would be alongside Robert Louis Stevenson and Captain Marryat as a writer of boys' adventure tales. For the novel proper, literary critics have long told us, must come to grips with reality; it should do more than merely tell a story. By this token, even the short *Silas Marner* can claim to be a novel, whereas *Treasure Island* is a yarn. Presumably, it was E. M. Forster's interest in what lay behind plot that led him to lament its necessity. Similarly, Edmund Gosse said about Stevenson that the 'literary atmosphere' was not in Samoa, but 'within a three-mile radius of Charing Cross'. He meant that in fiction, events take on deeper meaning, not in exotic surroundings, but in great cities, at social and political levels.

Now it cannot be denied that Conrad was attracted by the lushly romantic. If we think of two short romantic stories written before 1900—*Karain* and *The Lagoon*—Gosse's remark is not as fatuous as it at first seems. In an ironically critical moment, Conrad wrote of the first as a tale 'with the usual forests—river—stars—wind—sunrise—and so on—and lots of second-hand Conradese in it' (*Joseph Conrad: Life and Letters* I, 194). And he was liable to write in this vein throughout his career, particularly when Malaya was the inspiration. *Freya of the Seven Islands*, written after the chief masterpieces in 1912, represents such a lapse. So does *The Planter of Malata* (1914). It is a better story, but its fundamental contrivedness may be sensed by reading the last paragraph. The 'black', 'mournful', and 'mysterious' scene suggests 'anguish', and lowers the curtain on the trite memory of 'the heart that was broken there' (85–6).

Three things distinguish Conrad's best work from these excesses. The first is the fact that, unlike Hawthorne, he regarded violence as part of 'the ordinary course of man's experience'. This is well illustrated by his impressionistic treatment of Verloc's murder in *The Secret Agent*. First there is Verloc's unsuspecting wooing note as he tries to gain his wife's approval; next, the shadow of 'an arm with a clenched hand holding a carving knife'; then, the realisation that his wife has gone 'murdering mad'; and finally, his fleeting and futile plan to dash behind the table, though as it turns out he has time to move neither hand nor foot.

> Into that plunging blow, delivered over the side of the couch, Mrs. Verloc had put all the inheritance of her immemorial and obscure descent, the simple ferocity of the age of caverns, and the unbalanced nervous fury of the age of bar-rooms.   263

This sentence, with its linking of modern bar-room and primitive cavern, implies Conrad's belief in the continuing 'ferocity' of man down the ages. He adds:

> To the last . . . decorum had remained undisturbed by unseemly shrieks and other misplaced sincerities of conduct. And after the striking of the blow, this respectability continued in immobility and silence.   264

Sincerity, we are thus given to understand, has been prevented from breaking through. Middle-class respectability has checked any expression of the essential melodrama of the event. Conrad is not indulging in violence for its own sake; he is examining a trend of early twentieth-century society, a trend coming from the basic nature of man.

In the second place, it is only when he surrenders uncritically to the heightened moments that Conrad spoils them. At his best, he is highly suspicious of any romantic glamourising. It was an incurably romantic outlook that betrayed Lord Jim into his jump from the 'Patna', and in *Heart of Darkness* the foolish young trader who is so misguided as to worship Kurtz, does so because 'glamour left him unscathed' (126). What he lacked was Marlow's own cool and appraising eye. Given a more sceptical attitude he would have seen through the glamour to the reality.

Thirdly, Conrad often offsets his most exotic scenes by minutely observed and sordid details. He does this effectively in his first novel. After the long-drawn-out departure of Nina and Dain (*Almayer's Folly*, chapter XII), Almayer goes into Lingard's office. His vague thoughts of memory, death and eternity threaten a continuation of the 'second-hand Conradese' already given to the lovers. But as his eyes wander from the grimy books with their torn pages to the broken office desk and dusty shelves, the scene gains conviction (198). It is the sort of contrast needed more often throughout the book, and provided more effectively in the later works. The end of *Victory*, for example, would have seemed far too elaborately romanticised without the last short section. It is an abrupt change from the shuddering of the lurid storm and from Lena's exultant 'flush of rapture'. Seen through the laconic Davidson's eyes, 'the mystery of Samburan' becomes quite ordinary—Heyst is 'a queer chap', Jones and Ricardo two 'card-sharping rascals', and the terrible night just ended is no more than 'one of those silly thunderstorms that hang about the volcano'. It is the same in *Heart of Darkness*. On the one hand there is the seduction of the savage life all around; on the other, Marlow's routine tasks—bandaging the leaky steam pipes and supervising the native fireman who would otherwise be 'clapping his hands and stamping his feet' with the rest of those hidden in the jungle (97). In fact, keeping the ship going is Marlow's safeguard against 'peering' into 'creepy thoughts'; it represents his hold on sanity.

Henry James thought much about this matter of romance and reality. He found on re-reading *The American* that it had more aspects of a romance than he suspected. Yet he enjoyed it. In a typical Preface, full of careful definitions and of hesitations over too obvious formulations, he arrives at this conclusion: that the best novels do not offer the reader either romance or reality, but a current of both, 'extraordinarily rich and mixed'. So in Conrad. The 'shallow waters and forest-clad islands' of the east stand side by side with those scrap heaps and informal masses of rust that Marlow 'abominates'.

IMPERFECTIONS OF PLOT

Generally speaking, critics have not been able to offer better principles for plotting novels than Aristotle suggested for drama. Plots should have beginnings, middles and ends. Once the story has started, it should proceed probably, the events following one another naturally.

Judged from this standpoint, Conrad did not organise his plots well. Too often he delayed the action while he painted a scene or analysed a character; or he was guilty of over-complication or of obtrusive symbolism. His chief difficulties were caused by his inability to plan his novels in advance. Both *Lord Jim* and *The Secret Agent* were intended initially to be short stories; both took control of him until they became quite long novels. In fact, many of Conrad's endings seem hurried and unsatisfactory. For instance, the last section of *Nostromo* fails to match the magnificent presentation of Costaguana that has gone before. The reader's attention is surprisingly directed towards Nostromo's relationship with the two girls at the lighthouse, until the hero (his earlier deeds almost forgotten) is despatched by old Giorgio's bullet. And Heyst's burning of himself at the end of *Victory* is almost comic—'I suppose you are certain that Baron Heyst is dead?' 'He is ashes, Your Excellency'.

Robert Louis Stevenson was a far better teller of tales than Conrad. This is not surprising. He admitted (in *A Humble Remonstrance*, 1884) that in order to achieve a plot so carefully constructed 'that every incident is an illustration of the motive', he was prepared to sacrifice 'a thousand qualities'. Conrad was not so prepared and that is one reason why he is a more important novelist. His main concern was not with plot. It was, according to the Author's Note to *Typhoon and Other Stories,* with the effect of the events on the persons involved; and Conrad claims that he has tried to invest the story of *Typhoon* with a 'deeper significance' than any mere 'bit of a sea yarn' would have.

This search for significance, for a full and true presentation of his imagined world, makes Conrad a painter of individual scenes rather than a master of the long plot. The best of these scenes draw meaning from what has gone before and from what is to come after. In *Nostromo,* the fully realised blackness of the Golfo Placido is, for example, linked in our minds to events that happened before Conrad took the story up (to the death of Charles Gould's father among other things); it will still be in our minds as we watch Decoud die many pages later. In between the two events is another long scene—that between Doctor Monygham and Nostromo with the dead Hirsch as their only witness. And this is the way Conrad's novels are built up, by impressive scenes and less impressive linkings of them. The result is that his most effective plots are those of his shorter tales where there is less linking to be done. Hence the compact strength of *The Nigger, Typhoon, The Secret Sharer* and *The Shadow Line,* all of which are extended short stories. The last-named shows Conrad at his best in control of plot. Ford would have praised its *'progression d'effet'* (a term used by modern critics too). It means the technique of evolving an inevitable climax from a build-up of events; it is a kind of focus into which the whole story is drawn, and *The Shadow Line* is a fine example of it.

'THE SHADOW LINE'

The story is told autobiographically. The central theme of the hero's first 'ill-starred command' is introduced by an account of a scheme to prevent him from obtaining it; it is concluded by his report of the voyage to the man who had helped him to gain the appointment. The tale is thus neatly framed within a prologue and epilogue.

Events follow each other chronologically. The hero throws up an excellent job; survives an intrigue; reaches his ship and first mate (who had himself hoped to become captain); finds his ship becalmed, apparently indefinitely; learns gradually the full extent of the late captain's wickedness and madness; sees almost all his crew fall ill; but at last, in a rush, brings his ship safely to port. These are the bare bones of the story.

It is invested with a mysterious sense of inevitable doom. Thus, seemingly unimportant details of the opening (such as the perfection of the ship he is leaving, and the double meaning of 'carried me off' and other expressions) are ironic contrasts to the later nightmare (5). From the start, too, there is the sense that events can move only in one direction. Even so, Conrad gives his reader continual surprises. He does this through carefully placed and increasingly exciting climaxes—the lack of quinine, the weird but dramatic incident of the sick first mate's effort to shave, his subsequent madness and Ransome's risk in joining in the heavy work.

All is done with a fine hold on reality which owes a great deal to the descriptions of the routine tasks of shipboard. The tale therefore contains within the bounds of complete credibility, Burns's obsession with the evil influence of the late captain. The sentences are short, matching the economy of incident, and the conversation briskly sensible. The story has a natural rhythm, opening very slowly, picking up as the new captain goes to take charge of his ship, slowing down to the fixity of a bad dream during the long becalming and then, after the sudden drama of 'the darkness turning into water', moving with energy as the breeze blows. The undertone of grim humour even gives way to a moment of fun near the end when the surgeon who has now boarded the ship cries 'Heavens, what's that?' as the chief officer walks by (127). By way of conclusion, Ransome, who has performed so nobly, leaves the ship—'I am in a blue funk about my heart, Sir'. As he goes up the companion stairs, 'it was his hard fate to carry consciously within his faithful breast' the fear of sudden death (133).

This well-told story is both credible and exciting. It wins the reader's sympathy for the young captain. This is natural because he tells his own tale many years afterwards, and he looks back with sympathy and understanding at his former self. He notes that before his first command he lived 'in all the beautiful continuity of hope' (3), and that his throwing up of his first mate's berth was apparently very silly. As the tale gets under way, comments of this kind cease. The reader forgets the older man and stands beside the younger one, watching his bearing under the strain of his atrocious ill luck. The voyage takes on the air of an initiation ceremony, a trial of manhood. To the sensitive reader it is important that the captain retains full control of himself and therefore of those under his command.

The voyage over, Conrad very skilfully suggests an assessment of it. To most of us, the easy way of doing this would have been to get the narrator to make a comment from the wisdom of his greater experience, just as he does at the start. Instead, Conrad continues to present his story through the young captain's eyes: the reader remains in the present tense of the tale.

'What is this I hear?' asks Captain Giles, who had been responsible for the first command, 'Twenty-one days from Bankok?' (131).

The young captain treats him to a full account of the ordeal just ended. Thinking of the effect the responsibility has had on him, he concludes it by saying, 'All of you on shore look to me just a lot of skittish youngsters that have never known a care in the world'. Captain Giles considers this and makes two separate comments on it: 'one must not make too much of anything in life, good or bad', and 'a man should stand up to his bad luck, to his mistakes, to his conscience'. These comments are Conrad's way of suggesting an attitude to the story; he is warning his young captain (i) that dramatising individual events is unwise and (ii) that a man should accept with quiet determination whatever befalls him. Captain Giles follows these pieces of advice with a question: 'You aren't faint-hearted?'. This allows the younger man to move away from the self-pity of his earlier long account of his misfortunes into the genuine modesty of his reply of 'God only knows'. And when he adds, without any prompting, that he 'will be off at daylight to-morrow', Captain Giles grunts approvingly, 'That's the way. You'll do'. By which Conrad means his reader to understand that the narrator has come through his test successfully—that is, with courage and humility. But it is not a victory won for all time, for when the two men part on the note that 'there's precious little rest in life for anybody' (132), we take this to mean that life is made up of such tests; and when, to end the story, the narrator says good-bye to Ransome, who is seeking work on shore because of his bad heart, we are reminded that the final shadow line of death itself awaits us all.

Conrad had at first intended calling the story 'First Command'. The later title fitted better the presenting of the change from carefree youth to 'the more self-conscious and more poignant period of maturer life'. We cannot say, however, that Conrad has given his tale a moral, or that the events symbolise something else. That would be to make it not a story but a sermon or an allegory. We cannot say either that the meaning of the tale is explained by Captain Giles in the section dealt with above. That would reduce it to a narrative ending with an explanation. What we can say is that Conrad has controlled his story so well that it has taken on a universal significance. His art has invested the particular experience at the heart of *The Shadow Line* with the mysterious appeal which ensures that all readers recognise in it their own experience. It is not an experience which men encounter once only; each test of character has its own shadow line.

We said earlier that Conrad's main concern was not with plot. In the sense that he is doing more than telling a story, this is true. If it suggests that he achieves his full purpose by any method other than through his plot, it is not. *The Shadow Line* is so handled that in it everything is meant to throw light on the new captain's ordeal and its effect on him. Captain Giles's final Olympian view does in one way have a special significance. That is because it follows the climax of the story, at a point when, with the main excitement over, the reader is ready to hold the entire thing in his mind, savouring and assessing it. Captain Giles prompts this assessment, but what he says remains part of the whole pattern of the presentation of one event in a man's life, an event which brought him from the callowness of youth to the maturity of leadership. As we read of the event, it suggests (unconsciously perhaps) similar events which we and all men have experienced. This is the appeal of the work of art; and, as with all works of art, what it says and what it means are inseparable—the story is the meaning.

THE CHARACTERS

Aristotle had no doubt that in tragedy plot was more important than character. It is a view that could be applied also to such novelists as Fielding and Smollett. But in this century, serious novels have concerned themselves more with character and less with plot.

Novels in which plot is all-important are often content to indicate character by a kind of shorthand. Names like Allworthy (the squire in *Tom Jones*) invite, and gain, a stock response from the reader. When Fielding introduces him (chapter II) he does so briefly, indicating his 'agreeable person, sound constitution, solid understanding and benevolent heart'. There follows a summary of his earlier life and of his present domestic arrangements with his sister, Miss Bridget Allworthy.

If we compare this with the start of Virginia Woolf's *To the Lighthouse*, we find a very great difference. James Ramsey, a young boy, is sitting on the floor cutting pictures out of an illustrated catalogue. He is, we learn, one of those who 'cannot keep this feeling separate from that'. On hearing some good news, therefore, he endows the pictures in his magazine 'with heavenly bliss'. His inner life (or 'private code', as it is called) does not accord at all with his severe and frowning expression.

Joseph Conrad at the age of twenty-six

Joseph Conrad. Bust by Jacob Epstein

And, since we as yet know nothing of what Fielding would have called James's station in life, our impression of him is vague and fluid. All that we can be certain of is that we have here no stock character like Uriah Heep with his repeated 'very 'umble' and his fishy hands. We have, instead, the working of an introspective mind, the presentation of a state of consciousness—something that held little interest for either Fielding or Dickens.

Like Virginia Woolf, Conrad avoided the stock or flat character. Oddly enough, Simenon, the French detective writer who created Maigret, has praised and tried to emulate this aspect of Conrad's work. In an interview given to the *Paris Review* (it can be found in *Writers at Work*, ed. Cowley), Simenon said that he aimed to make his characters three-dimensional, like carvings in wood. They would then be 'brothers of everybody in the world'—a goal 'more like a poet's goal' than that of a novelist. Gogol, according to Simenon, had succeeded in doing this. He made characters like everyday people and gave them a third dimension, a 'poetic aura'. This aura 'comes naturally'; it is 'the kind Conrad has', it gives characters the 'weight of sculpture' (143).

Peyrol, the hero of *The Rover*, is a good example of what Simenon is describing. He has all the elements of a fabular figure. Having lost his real name, he has been given a new one during his mysterious and largely forgotten childhood. He has lived excitingly and bravely, in exotic parts of the world, often at odds with authority, and he owns a chest, full of who-knows-what treasure trove. He carries on his person, sewn into a weird waistcoat, a mass of foreign coins worth sixty or seventy thousand francs. This money, Conrad informs us, is enough—

> to justify his flight of fancy, while looking at the countryside in the light of the sunset, that what he had on him would buy all that soil from which he had sprung: houses, woods, vines, olives, vegetable gardens, rocks and salt lagoons—in fact, the whole landscape, including the animals in it. 12

This is the kind of sentence that we might expect to find in a fairy tale by Hans Andersen. It makes Peyrol larger-than-life and gives him (the lowest born) a magic control over the world.

By no means all Conrad's characters have that, but a surprisingly large number of them have legendary qualities. Heyst on his lonely island, Kurtz, hidden deep in Africa, and Leggatt (of *The Secret Sharer*) appearing suddenly and mysteriously out of the sea, are all solitary figures, rooted in no past, committed to an uncertain future. Almayer, we remember, Conrad's first hero, was another legend, a man he first learned of on other men's lips:

> Your name was the common property of the winds: it, as it were, floated naked over the waters about the Equator. I wrapped round its unhonoured form the royal mantle of the tropics and have essayed to put into the hollow sound the very anguish of paternity.   A PERSONAL RECORD, 88

Conrad did not try to depict him as he was. He 'wrapped him round' with a mantle, which corresponds, presumably, to Simenon's third dimension; and the effort to make him symbolise paternity is the equivalent of Simenon's 'brother of everybody in the world'.

Conrad's mantle is a static symbol. It suggests a slow, formal presentation of character. Yet character is revealed in action, and action is movement. It is thus necessary to show that the still and dignified legendary figure is also an individual in action. So we get film-shots, as it were, of the larger-than-life heroes, often in moments of high drama. Chapter XVI of *The Rover* shows how Peyrol tricks Captain Vincent. At its climax, Peyrol's tiller is 'knocking about terribly under him', his tartane (boat) gives a 'desperate lurch', and his heart flies into his mouth. At this, his moment of death, he is engaged in violent action.

Ford said that such scenes rendered character. By this he meant that they are not generalised announcements by the author but realisations of character in action. He gives the following example (quoted on p. 40 of *The Rhetoric of Fiction*, by W. Booth):

> 'We knew that if we said: "Mr. X was a foul-mouthed reactionary", you would know very little about him. But if his

first words were: "God Damn it, put all the filthy Liberals up against a wall, say I, and shoot out their beastly livers . . .", that gentleman will make on you an impression that many following pages shall scarcely efface.'

The words indicate Conrad's method.

CHARACTER IN 'CHANCE' AND 'NOSTROMO'
Rendering character in action does not give fully-rounded characters. Michael Henchard in *The Mayor of Casterbridge* and Becky Sharp in *Vanity Fair* are vivid in a way in which Lord Jim and Lena are not. 'Rendering' suggests rather the contradictory complexity of human beings. There is an interesting section towards the end of chapter II of *Chance* where Marlow considers the effect on the very ordinary Fynes of the disappearance of Flora. Fyne is so ordinary that Marlow supposes the cutting of bread and butter to be the most dangerous activity he has ever undertaken, and tries to imagine his thoughts in the face of such a mysterious happening as flight. He does so because 'he had never really understood the Fynes'. There follows this paragraph:

> But when Fyne and I got back into the room, then in the searching, domestic glare of the lamp, inimical to the play of fancy, I saw these two stripped of every vesture it had amused me to put on them for fun. Queer enough they were. Is there a human being that isn't that—more or less secretly? But whatever their secret it was manifest to me that it was neither subtle nor profound. They were a good, stupid, earnest couple and very much bothered. They were that—with the usual unshaded crudity of average people. There was nothing in them that the lamplight might not touch without the slightest risk of indiscretion.
>
> 56, 57

Marlow is here trying to uncover the essential nature of the Fynes. He is aware that all men and women have, as it were, secret basic selves which are very hard to come at, and that his impressions of the Fynes have been wrong—a 'vesture put on them for fun'. But this new attempt to understand them more closely is no more successful than earlier ones, and they remain hidden from him, just average people who are upset.

This attempt to explore the real person is in Conrad a permanent endeavour. He has his own method of conducting it. He does not do it through deep thought. When the 'I' who is listening to the story of *Chance* remarks that Marlow seems to have studied de Barral closely, Marlow denies it. He asserts that 'a glimpse and no more' is the proper way of seeing 'an individuality' (84). A glimpse gives knowledge, which is 'a chance acquisition preserving in its repose a fine resonant quality'. Studying people gives only information, 'something one goes out to seek and puts away when found as you might do a piece of lead: ponderous, useful, unvibrating, dull' (88).

The glimpses Conrad affords us of his main characters have two purposes—to show how much they have in common with other men, and to emphasise their 'real' selves. An involuntary outburst by de Barral in *Chance* illustrates the first purpose. The financier's trial is a dull affair. In the main, he remains unmoved. When the prosecuting counsel (who has been harrying him) asks him if he likes cards, de Barral unexpectedly turns on him—'You yourself as well', he cries. 'Why, now I think of it, it took me most of my time to keep people, just of your sort, off me' (83).

Equally, the moment illustrates a side of de Barral we have not suspected. Marlow observes that it was 'as though the fact had dawned upon him for the first time'. De Barral's only other departure from the dull routine of the case was an instant towards the end of the trial when he raised a hard-clenched fist above his head. Marlow notes that the 'pressman' disapproved of this gesture, which did not fit in with the general, colourless tenor of his report. The fact leads Marlow to reflect that journalism (or bad art, as he might have said in a different context) deals only in pasteboard figures. Journalists are paid to write readable accounts. To be successful, they must be careful *not* to understand; otherwise, they would be led too far away from 'the actualities which are the daily bread of the public mind' (87). Marlow himself looked behind the gesture and was rewarded by an insight—that de Barral's imagination had been at last roused into activity. 'Just try', he says, 'to enter into the feelings of a man whose imagination wakes up' just before he is imprisoned (87).

Conrad's characters, then, are caught in moments when imagination informs their actions and are presented through the answering imagination of their creator. This is why so often their actions are unexpected.

Nostromo moves from expected to unexpected action. He is first seen through Mitchell who praises him as 'a man absolutely above reproach' (13). Mitchell claims that he is 'a pretty good judge of character', which is Conrad's ironic way of pointing out that Mitchell is like the pressmen in *Chance*. When we do see Nostromo for ourselves, he is still a type. He wears a superb costume and is 'got up with more finished splendour than any well-to-do ranchers of the Campo had ever displayed on a high holiday' (125). On the black gulf, when, along with Decoud, he is trying to make safe the silver, he at first behaves as his public reputation would lead us to expect. Then the façade crumbles and the real man is seen at last. We watch this happening through the mind of Decoud, who notes that Nostromo is not equal to the situation (282). 'Something deeper, something unexpected by everyone had come to the surface.' This unexpected aspect of the Capataz's character, seen and commented on by the sceptical Decoud, marks the break between his old, established life in Sulaco and his new restless movements between his yacht and the lighthouse.

In general Conrad's main characters are blurred. We approach them through the minds of others (Lord Jim as analysed by Marlow is the obvious example) or see them in glimpses that are very striking but strongly contrasted. Both these aspects of technique stem from unwillingness to make too clear a judgment. Room must be left for the imagination to blow where it lists and to move men in the most unlikely ways. When we read of Charles Gould in the early pages of *Nostromo* that he was 'spare and tall, with a gleaming moustache, a neat chin, clear blue eyes, auburn hair, and a thin fresh, red face' (46), we can be sure that

Conrad will complicate this plain statement before long. And he does. Gould's wife waxes indignant at Costaguanan life. 'My dear', her husband observes gently, 'you seem to forget that I was born there' (49). Conrad comments: 'These few words made her pause as if they had been a sudden revelation', and we meet again the unexpected, the reversal of an earlier impression.

THE MINOR CHARACTERS

When there are clear-cut figures in Conrad's work they are minor ones. This is understandable. Conrad still practises the technique of giving glimpses, but because these characters are on the fringe of stories, we see less of them, and there is no room for their development. Nikita in *Under Western Eyes* is a strikingly etched figure with only a small part in the story. He is introduced at the start of the fourth section of part III of the novel; and he is at first a typically shadowy Conrad figure— a man of legend, 'supposed to have killed more gendarmes and police agents than any revolutionist living', to 'have been innumerable times in and out of Russia' and to have 'lived between whiles (Razumov had heard) on the shores of the Lake of Como, with a charming wife devoted to the cause, and two young children' (266–7). Yet when he acts and speaks, the legend proves a lie. With his flabby body and squeaky voice, he is anything but the silent and ruthless revolutionary. He is almost a caricature.

Then, at the end of the book, he reveals his true self when he inflicts deafness on Razumov.

> Before he had time to turn round and confront them fairly, they set on him with a rush. He was driven head-long against the wall. 'I wonder how', he completed his thought. Nikita cried, with a shrill laugh right in his face, 'We shall make you harmless. You wait a bit.'
>
> Razumov did not struggle. The three men held him pinned against the wall, while Nikita, taking up a position a little on one side, deliberately swung off his enormous arm. Razumov, looking for a knife in his hand, saw it come at him open, unarmed, and received a tremendous blow on the side of his head

over his ear. At the same time he heard a faint, dull detonating sound, as if someone had fired a pistol on the other side of the wall. A raging fury awoke in him at this outrage . . . Razumov, overpowered, breathless, crushed under the weight of his assailants, saw the monstrous Nikita squatting on his heels near his head, while the other held him down, kneeling on his chest, gripping his throat, lying across his legs.

'Turn his face the other way', the paunchy terrorist directed, in an excited, gleeful squeak. 368–9

It is a scene (with a tailpiece at the end of section IV) which makes Nikita one of Conrad's most striking minor characters, both cowardly and larger-than-life ('monstrous'). The fact that he turns out to be a scoundrel of the worst kind—'a traitor himself, a betrayer—a spy' —only heightens our horror.

The danger with such a minor character is that he may become a type, for not even Conrad can unfailingly seek out the imaginative moment which reveals the true secret of a man's character. There is a gallery of these types in *Victory*: Gentleman Jones, Ricardo, Pedro, Schomberg and his wife. Ricardo is a stage villain with sunken eyes, a quick grin that shows his teeth, a hollow voice and a knife up the leg of his trousers. Heyst speaks of him and Jones in this way: 'Here they are before you, [Lena] —evil intelligence, instinctive savagery arm in arm.' They are not individuals but forces typified, and their vividness, even though it approaches caricature, creates an illusion of reality lacking in the much more shadowy Heyst and Lena.

Conrad once gave Galsworthy the following advice:

In a book you should love the idea and be scrupulously faithful to your conception of life. There lies the honour of the writer, not in the fidelity to his personages. You must never allow them to decoy you out of yourself. As against your people you must preserve an attitude of perfect indifference, the part of creative power.

JOSEPH CONRAD: LIFE AND LETTERS I, 301

The words tell us that Conrad was not primarily interested in the creation of character. We must not look in his work for a

Julien Sorel or Mr. Micawber. We must look instead for an 'idea', a 'conception of life'. The characters will not exist as profound portraits or remarkable photographs. Fidelity of this kind is an irrelevance. The first thing about a novel is its total statement, its vision of life. In this the characters will play their part, but it is only a part.

CONRAD'S WOMEN

The women in Conrad's novels are vague for quite a different reason. They are sentimentalised. They represent a weakness in Conrad very similar to that which F. R. Leavis complained of in George Eliot when, in *The Great Tradition*, he argued that she cannot separate herself from the 'soul hunger', the hazy indefiniteness of such characters as Dorothea in *Middlemarch* and Maggie in *The Mill on The Floss*. So it is, Leavis tells us, that in a great novelist, 'her own immature self' exists side by side with 'the genius that is self-knowledge'.

In Conrad, *The Arrow of Gold* represents only 'the immature self'. Its theme is Doña Rita, Conrad's first love, and its setting, the Marseilles he had known in his youth. Conrad is more concerned with confession of his youth than with the novel as an art form. The natural reticence which prevents him from parading his soul in public leads to hints and indirections. These are not (as they are in Conrad's best work) the result of the complexity of his vision of life; they stem from the fact that he is too involved in the events he is describing. 'There are some of these 42-years-old episodes', he told Colvin, 'of which I cannot think now without a slight tightness in the chest' (*Joseph Conrad: Life and Letters* II, 229). Hence, perhaps, the artificially contrived and pointlessly enigmatic nature of much of the dialogue. This is a fair example:

> 'You set up for being unforgiving', she said without anger. I sprang to my feet while she turned about and came towards me bravely, with a wistful smile on her bold, adolescent face. 'It seems to me', she went on in a voice like a wave of love itself, 'that one should try to understand before one sets up for being

unforgiving. Forgiveness is a very fine word. It is a fine invocation.'

'There are other fine words in the language such as fascination, fidelity, also frivolity; and as for invocations there are plenty of them too. For instance, alas, Heaven help me.'

We stood very close together, her narrow eyes were as enigmatic as ever, but that face, which, like some ideal conception of art, was incapable of anything like untruth and grimace, expressed by some mysterious means such a depth of infinite patience that I felt profoundly ashamed of myself.   222

And Monsieur George's own romantic commentary is often worse. No wonder that, thinking of the whole story, Conrad asked himself whether 'anyone could have rendered its ominous glow, its atmosphere of exultation and misery'. Like his own curé considering Arlette (*The Rover*), he assumed too readily that woman was 'the symbolic figure of spiritual mystery'. And just as George Eliot failed to hold at arm's length the tremulous yearnings of young lovers, and, by identifying herself too closely with them, betrayed parts of her novels into sentimental softness, so Conrad, his scepticism suspended when handling very much the same theme, fell into mawkish and wordy evocations.

It is not just *The Arrow of Gold* that was marred in this way; many of the greater works are flawed by the sentimentality of the women. Lena, in *Victory*, is presented to us at the start of part II, through Heyst's consciousness. He is idly watching the orchestra of which she is a member and in this mood becomes vaguely aware of a dress and a pair of small hands, attached to well-folded arms. The sight of two thick brown tresses of hair leads him to the mental exclamation—'A girl, by Jove!' (70). He studies her more closely and positively forgets where he is— he loses touch with his surroundings. And once glimpsed in this way, Lena never regains firm touch with the world of the novel. We are told only isolated details of her earlier life (that a nasty old lady who lived in Camberwell interpreted dreams for a shilling), and when we do see her in fuller scenes (such as in the search for the missing revolver, section IX), it is Heyst, not Lena, that we are mainly concerned with. She thus remains 'immobile' and 'statuesque', exemplifying, as in a dream, the 'charm of art tense with life'. These words are Conrad's own. They suggest a serious failure in communication. Conrad is investing femininity with an aura of sacred distance. His women, just because they are women, are set apart. Their unreality is to be reverenced. So Lena remains a shadowy, sentimental figure.

Arlette in *The Rover* is similar, an idealised conception with carmine lips, and pellucid unfathomable black eyes. As with so many of Conrad's women (Flora in *Chance*, Natalie in *Under Western Eyes* or Jewel in *Lord Jim*) she is rootless and unprotected in a hostile world. Conrad attempts to account for her frozen timidity—for the fact that at the start of the novel she is, in her own words, 'not alive at all'—by giving us to understand that she was too closely involved in the bloodshed of the Revolution (90–2). The effort is not very successful, but that Conrad made it at all, suggests that he was aware of the danger of having yet another misty heroine.

Generally speaking, when we meet Conrad's women we move into the realm of magazine romance where the conventional and romantic emotion is suggested by the conventional and overworked word. Too few of Conrad's heroines receive the belittling scrutiny of his irony. (Winnie Verloc in *The Secret Agent* is an outstanding exception.) Most of them walk in the heaven's embroidered cloths. In so doing, they reflect their creator's idealised conception of womanhood. No doubt, it was difficult for one who had scarcely known a mother's love, had then had the romantic idyll of his adolescence cut short and who had not married until he was forty, to look on woman with a cool appraising eye. Certainly in his novels, young love is nearly always a fairy tale played by a prince and princess. This may do at a pinch for Dain and Nina in their exotic Malayan setting. It will not do at all for Nostromo and Giorgio's daughter, or for Heyst and Lena.

7
Technique 2:
Point of View — Narration and Time

A novelist may tell his tale in either the first or third person. If he uses the first person, he can give in detail the 'I's' inner thoughts and feelings, though he will find the inner lives of the other characters less easy to present. If he uses the third person, he can, as nameless and all-knowing narrator, allow his characters to speak their thoughts aloud in order to inform us what they are individually thinking and feeling. This is called interior monologue.

Dickens, for example, uses a combination of these methods in *Bleak House*. E. M. Forster (in *Aspects of the Novel*) has called this 'bouncing', meaning that, without warning, the reader is switched from one method of story-telling to another. He notes that in chapter I Dickens is able to explain everyone who appears; in chapter II he is able to explain Sir Leicester Dedlock, his wife only partly, and Mr. Tulkinghorn not at all. Then, with surprising suddenness, he entrusts chapter III to Esther Summerson, who writes in the first person.

Conrad, too, uses a number of methods. *The Arrow of Gold* is told by 'I'; *The Rover* by an invisible narrator. *Nostromo* is largely presented by a narrator, but parts of it are seen through Decoud's journal and letters. Many other novels and short stories are 'told' by Marlow, a one-time sailor who is seen at the start as one of a number of men gathered together after dinner. Where Marlow is not used, there is often an equivalent narrator —Davidson in *Victory* and the teacher of languages in *Under Western Eyes*.

Percy Lubbock, less accommodating than E. M. Forster to the practice of novelists, states in his *Craft of Fiction* that the centrally important question in the technique of novel-writing is that of the relation of the novelist to the story he tells. He pays close attention to Flaubert, noting that he 'sometimes talks with his own voice, sometimes through one of the people in the book'. And he says that it is not easy for the novelist to talk in his own voice the whole time. To do so is to adopt the attitude of God towards the world created on the page.

If the novelist feels himself part of an ordered and stable society, and is writing a novel about a similarly ordered and stable world, he perhaps finds it easy to view his creation with the superior knowledge of God. In *Emma*, for example, Jane Austen's main concern is with a clear and limited theme: the learning by a young woman that it is conceited folly to try to arrange other people's matrimonial affairs for them. Now *Emma* is a good story. Jane Austen is very successful in persuading us of the reality of Highbury and its inhabitants. The reader may not notice, until it is pointed out, what is nevertheless a fact—that Emma learns her lesson in well-defined episodes (through Mr. Elton's proposal to herself, through her own interest in Frank Churchill, through her futile attempt to bring Harriet Smith and Frank Churchill together, and through Mr. Knightley's wisdom and love). These follow each other like mathematical gradations until the novel moves to an obvious climax, in which Emma admits that she was a 'fool' ever to attempt to interfere in the courtship of others. After this confession she is able to marry Mr. Knightley.

The advantages of this technique are that it makes the novel easy to follow. It also leaves us in no doubt about its moral implications. A serious disadvantage is that because Mr. Knightley is the main instrument of Emma's education, he tends to become a mouthpiece for sound moral precept, an abstraction like the Virtues and Vices in a Morality Play rather than a fully realised character.

Conrad had no such clear lesson to teach. The world in which his characters move is not the kind where lessons are learned so well that someone announces how foolish he has been and is thereafter fit to marry. It is not even the kind of world where anyone understands beyond doubt why Lord Jim jumped from the 'Patna' or why, at the start of *Under Western Eyes*, Razumov betrayed Haldin. It is full of ambiguities. Out of them was born Marlow.

MARLOW IN 'YOUTH'

Youth is the first tale in which Conrad uses Marlow. It seems on the face of it to offer the reader a simple, basic idea, one worked out more briefly and with much less complication of plot and character than *Emma*. It is a lyrical account of a young man's first voyage to the East. Although it is a short story and not an autobiographical record, it is based on Conrad's own voyage to Bangkok in the 'Palestine', a ship which underwent misfortunes very like the ones in *Youth*. The theme invites simple handling. Conrad wants to evoke the thrill of being young and of journeying to a romantic, far-off part of the world. What more is needed than to set down a straightforward story told in the first person?

Marlow does recount events chronologically. At the same time he makes highly poetic and frequent comments on the 'strength, faith and imagination of youth'. He acts as a kind of chorus, as in Greek tragedy. But he has other uses, too, and they result from Conrad's wish to distance himself from the experience behind the tale. If he identifies himself too closely with the young Marlow, he will abandon himself uncritically to the illusions of youth. He therefore looks at events through the eyes of a Marlow much older and wiser, who can recapture the flavour of his own youth and yet avoid sentimentality. He can also explore the nature and meaning of what befell him as a young man. For Marlow is aware of other aspects of youth than its magical excitement. It may have a glamour 'more dazzling than the flames of the burning ship'; yet it is 'more cruel, more pitiless, more bitter than the sea' (30). Marlow enables Conrad to state both points of view.

Youth opens with Conrad's own impression of the 'director of companies, accountant, lawyer, Marlow, and myself . . . gathered round a mahogany table'. It closes with Conrad's picture of the same men, nodding at Marlow—

> . . . over the polished table that like a still sheet of brown water reflected our faces, lined, wrinkled; our faces marked by toil, by deceptions, by success, by love; our weary eyes looking still, looking always, looking anxiously for something out of life, that while it is expected is already gone—has passed unseen, in a sigh, in a flash—together with the youth, with the strength, with the romance of illusions. 42

Are we meant to be looking directly at these faces or do we see them, as it were at a remove, reflected in the polished table? To Conrad, experience was as fleeting as the reflections in the table—no sooner expected than gone. Like the table, Marlow is a reflection; like the table, he reminds us that the external appearance is not the full reality.

MARLOW IN 'LORD JIM'

Lord Jim uses Marlow with greater complication. Conrad begins the story speaking as author. Then at the Court of Inquiry (the end of the fourth chapter) we find Jim's glance meeting the eyes of an observer who 'seemed to be aware of his hopeless difficulty' (33). The observer is Marlow, and he now takes over the tale. This is referred to again on pp. 110–111.

One immediate result is to involve us more sympathetically with Jim. 'It's easy enough to talk of Master Jim, after a good spread . . . with a box of decent cigars handy', says Marlow (35). The implication is that it is equally easy to sit in a comfortable chair and read about him, and that it would be a mistake to dismiss him lightly.

Another result is to heighten the drama. Here are a few sentences from the start of chapter X. Jim has just jumped from the 'Patna'.

> The sea hissed 'like twenty thousand kettles'. That's his simile, not mine . . . He crouched down in the bows and stole a furtive

glance back. He saw just one yellow gleam of the mast-head light high up and blurred like a last star ready to dissolve. 'It terrified me to see it still there', he said. That's what he said. What terrified him was the thought that the drowning was not over yet. No doubt he wanted to be done with that abomination as quickly as possible.   112

They are sentences more concerned with describing Jim's excited state of mind than his actions, and in this they effectively prolong the tensions of the novel's central event. Marlow's explanation of 'That's his simile, not mine' is completely successful in calling up in the reader a kind of wonderment at a dramatic comparison that would otherwise have passed unnoticed.

As the novel progresses, Marlow and Lord Jim become involved in a close personal relationship. Marlow ceases to be an observer and becomes a participant in Jim's fate. This further complicates the narration, forming a separate theme, parallel to the main events. Conrad uses it to control the pace of the story and also to condition the reader's attitude to Lord Jim: Marlow's understanding of him ebbs and flows according to the progress of their friendship. The following passage from the chapter last quoted shows this process at work:

> He tried to sound my thought with an attentive glance dropped on me in passing. 'Do you mean to say you had been deliberating with yourself whether you would die?' I asked in as impenetrable a tone as I could command. He nodded without stopping. 'Yes, it had come to that as I sat there alone', he said. He passed on a few steps to the imaginary end of his beat, and when he flung round to come back both his hands were thrust deep in his pockets. He stopped short in front of my chair and looked down. 'Don't you believe it?' he inquired with intense curiosity. I was moved to make a solemn declaration of my readiness to believe implicitly anything he thought fit to tell me.   126–7

This little scene with Marlow is of the utmost importance to Jim. It bears on the idea announced in the Novalis quotation on the title-page: 'It is certain my Conviction gains infinitely, the moment another soul will believe in it.' In fact, this aspect of the novel is developed almost entirely through the deepening relationship of Marlow and Jim.

We must not, however, make the mistake of judging Jim only through Marlow. To do this would be to replace the all-seeing, God-like intelligence of Jane Austen's nameless narrator by a similar but less impressive figure—less impressive because Marlow has been described in detail and given human frailty as well as wisdom. To avoid this, Conrad introduces another observer, Stein. He was not present at the trial, but Marlow (to quote what are on this occasion lame words) 'considered him an eminently suitable person to receive my confidences about Jim's difficulties' (203).

Stein tells Marlow of his capture of a rare butterfly for his collection; Marlow replies: 'I came here to describe a specimen . . .' It is 'nothing so perfect' as a butterfly, but a man. Stein becomes grave. 'Ach, so!', he says. 'Well—I am a man too' (211–12). He proceeds to diagnose and prescribe for Jim's plight. These paragraphs (chapter XX) are among the best-known in the book, because they seem to suggest the right attitude, the 'meaning' of the whole business. Stein speaks like this: 'Jim is romantic—romantic. And that is very bad . . . Very good, too' (216).

These enigmatic words show the danger Conrad is in. There is a point in elaboration beyond which he cannot usefully go. The reader should not accept unreservedly Marlow's comments —fair enough. He is then given Stein's view of affairs—and it turns out to be a mysterious compound of opposites broken occasionally by a few German or Latin words—'that was the way. To follow the dream, and again to follow the dream—and so—ewig—usque ad finem . . .' (214–15). The phrases are too vague and puzzling. As an introduction to Jim's life in Patusan they complicate further what is already complicated enough. The second half of the novel becomes increasingly indirect. Jim's struggle with Brown and consequent death are not revealed until 'more than two years later'. A thick packet arrives containing not one account, but three: Marlow's long narrative, a

hung brighter than a
mass of silver in the
moonlight, in that cry
of a longing heart
sending its never ceasing
vibration into a sky
empty of stars, the
genius of the magnificent
Capataz de Cargadores
dominated the place.

The End

30th Aug. 1904

Stanford-le-Hope

Last page of the first draft of *Nostromo*

The *Otago*, Conrad's first command

letter from Jim to his father, and a shorter letter of exhortation from Marlow (chapter XXVI).

MARLOW IN 'CHANCE'

It is with Marlow as with any other method of narration used in a novel: the result is both gain and loss. *Lord Jim* is inconceivable without him. So is *Heart of Darkness*, where his function is to convey the horror of the seductive power of the jungle and its natives, though in this story, too, he has his shortcoming (chiefly of wordiness)

In *Chance* his role is less successful. At first, a certain Powell describes his early sailing career. Marlow is one of his audience. When Powell mentions the 'Ferndale', Marlow is able to join in and begin the story of the heroine, Flora de Barral. But much of his information about her is at second or third hand. Henry James said (in an essay 'The New Novel') that information reached the reader like water in buckets passed down a chain of men trying to put out a fire; and he complained that some water was inevitably spilt. It is spilt in two ways: the story becomes confused, and its implications blurred.

Conrad may have recognised this, for he did not repeat the excessive elusiveness of *Chance*. Nor did he ever find it easy to deal with Marlow at the end of a story; the return to the scene round the dinner-table can easily be an anticlimax. But even in the later, more straightforward novels, Conrad remained unwilling to commit himself to obvious or simple readings of human behaviour. Which of us knows how our mind works, or why we have acted in a particular way? Perhaps the best we can do is to probe, not towards the full answer, but towards a hint of it. Marlow is one of Conrad's methods of attempting this.

UNORDERED PICTURES

Time was one of the problems of novel-writing which Conrad and Ford discussed together. In *Joseph Conrad: A Personal Rememberance*, Ford has left a statement of their agreement about the inadequacy of straightforward, chronological sequence:

A novel must therefore not be a narrative, a report. Life does not say to you: in 1914, my next door neighbour, Mr. Slack, erected a greenhouse and painted it with Cox's green aluminium paint. . . . If you think about the matter you will remember, in various unordered pictures, how one day Mr. Slack appeared in his garden and contemplated the wall of his house. You will then try to remember the year of that occurrence and will fix it as August 1914 because having had the foresight to bear the municipal stock of the city of Liège, you were able to afford a first class season ticket for the first time in your life. You will remember Mr. Slack—then much thinner because it was before he found out. At this point you will remember that you were then the manager of the fresh fish branch of Messrs. Catlin and Clovis in Fenchurch Street. What a change since then! Millicent had not yet put her hair up . . . (etc. etc.).   180–81

Perhaps the simplest use of the break in time-sequence is to reveal some exciting happening which has been kept hidden from the characters and readers alike. A clear instance of this can be found in *Vanity Fair*. In the early chapters Thackeray has recounted Becky Sharp's schooling and early days with Amelia. It is all done in a very straightforward way, the more so because the 'dear reader' has been consulted, taken on one side, admitted to confidences, and generally made to feel very important. He watches Becky set her cap at a number of men. It seems that even that old boor, Sir Pitt Crawley, is smitten. In fact, he proposes to Becky. And great is his surprise and great is the reader's to hear Becky's confession that 'she is married already'. The words make a positively melodramatic ending to a chapter. That is why Thackeray places them there.

This is not the kind of thing Ford means, although it is good entertainment. It is not the kind of thing Conrad practises, either. *The Secret Agent*, for example, makes no attempt to reveal suddenly, after the manner of Thackeray announcing Becky's marriage, the identity of Stevie's murderer. Both the police and the reader know this quite early in the story. And if Conrad does show a dramatic confrontation, as in *Nostromo* where the hero appears before old Giorgio who supposes him dead (468), the reader is well prepared for it—he has been with Nostromo since his swim to the Isabels. The interest here is not in the mere event but in the minds of the two men. Both are fashioning new lives, one without his wife, the other without his honourable public image. Their exchanges have a prolonged tension that is far more powerful than any trickery with the plot.

When Conrad does use surprise it is with a serious purpose. His use of the sudden revelation of an earlier moment of time (flash-back, as it is called) illustrates this. Early in *Typhoon* Conrad mentions Captain MacWhirr's impulsive flight from his father's Belfast grocery store (4). It is totally at variance with his unimaginative and stolid behaviour during the rest of the story, and its purpose is to suggest that there are curious contradictions in even naïve, straightforward men like MacWhirr. It prevents the reader from making a hurried, superficial judgment of character.

In *Victory*, a similar unexpected glimpse of the past dramatises the fact that Heyst's head and heart are pulling in opposite directions. Just after he has helped Lena, Conrad shows him years earlier with his dying father. 'Look on', his father advises him; 'make no sound' (175)—he has found by bitter experience that involvement with others brings suffering and disillusionment. The younger Heyst accepts this; he determines to make his life a 'masterpiece' of aloofness. Yet Conrad has just shown him as an older man betrayed by his sympathy into befriending a lonely and unhappy girl. The juxtaposition of the two scenes highlights the opposing forces in Heyst's life.

The breaking of the normal time-sequence is, in fact, an effective and economical method of conditioning the reader's attitude to the novels. Chronologically, the events of *Lord Jim* occur in this order: The 'Patna's' voyage, its mysterious accident, Jim's desertion, the Court of Inquiry, and Jim's ultimate job as a dogged, self-assertive water-clerk. But Conrad starts with the clerk, a good worker who 'nevertheless with black ingratitude would throw up the job suddenly and depart' (4). Then the book's third paragraph begins by admitting that Jim has been working incognito—to hide 'not a personality but a fact' (4); and it was when the fact was discovered that he always left.

Why did Conrad begin his story at a moment in time when the enquiry was over and Jim was trying to live down his past? Since, as we now know, Conrad at first intended *Lord Jim* to be a short story, and added and developed Jim's career in Patusan only later, we may say that Conrad is starting at the end. This is because by so doing he can leave the reader with a vivid impression of the calamity that has overtaken his hero. The first glimpse of the immaculate but haunted Jim ensures that the tale will be dominated by the idea of his disgrace. Conrad wants to leave the reader in no doubt that the one thing a man must not do is to lose his honour, and the opening unforgettable image of Jim is a very effective way of achieving this end.

In the words quoted at the start of this section, Ford claims that in real life, people considering the present are aware of the past and perhaps of the future too. According to this view, events do not overtake men in neat parcels of time; they unfold partially, involving as many areas of time as they do people. Conrad's most complicated novels aim at giving this impression.

E. M. Tilyard puts this well. Writing of *Nostromo* (in *The Epic Strain in the English Novel*), he says:

> Conrad's greatest triumph . . . is that he creates the illusion of life being lived all at once by a great number of very different people. He does this partly by his technique of passing backward and forward in time, thereby removing from the reader all temptation to thin out events by stringing them on a long chain. 157

It is a technique employed from the earliest pages. The Golfo Placido is called up, the distant Azuera Mountains and the port of Sulaco. Human beings, we are led to think, are not of much account in this land of legends which go back to the beginning of human records. We are measuring time in centuries. Captain Mitchell enters with his self-important account of the latest revolution. As he talks we learn of both the past and the present;

he refers casually to names which will eventually bulk large in our story—Nostromo is one of them. Then we meet the Goulds. Again we move to and fro in time, now with Gould's father, now during his courtship in Italy, now in Costaguana where his married life is being destroyed by the mine. When Decoud appears, it is the same. His journal takes us into the past even as he lives out the present.

This suggestion of the flow of life carries with it an insight into the implications of events. They are implications no more logical or even clear than in real life. Conrad seems deliberately to avoid logical sequence. In *Victory*, Lena's flight with Heyst is revealed in a bewildering way. It is hinted at early in the book. Davidson (the rather unlikely narrator who is so often conveniently at hand on the disused pier of the Tropical Trading Company) mentions it to Mrs. Schomberg. At this moment we hardly know who Lena is. Conrad then shows her mild persecution as a member of the Zangiacomo orchestra. After this Schomberg speaks of her flight, reveals both his own designs upon her and his absurd view of Heyst as a wealthy and unscrupulous perverter of young girls; and then implicates the sinister Jones in pursuit of the couple. In fact, we see the effect of the flight on others, not the flight itself. And as far as Heyst and Lena are concerned, we find out what has happened only fragmentarily—we look on through the irony of recollections of Heyst's father's advice to take no part in life, and of Lena's aunt's life in London. The action has become like a web; those involved interweave their parts and we watch from different angles and moments of time.

TIME IN 'CHANCE'

Of all Conrad novels, *Chance* is the most elaborately indirect, particularly in its handling of time. Part I offers a good field for analysis and for commenting on some of the advantages and disadvantages of Conrad's narrative method.

Its basic story is quite simple. The heroine, Flora de Barral, is the daughter of a very wealthy financier, a widower, who is gaoled after his bankruptcy when she is still little more than a child. The housekeeper and servants employed to look after her desert her, and she stays with a number of people, including the Fynes, acquaintances of Marlow. She is so miserable that she twice attempts suicide. The first time she meets Marlow, the second time Mrs. Fyne's brother, Captain Anthony. The two elope.

Conrad does not tell the story in this direct way. The first chapter shows us Marlow and his audience in 'a riverside inn'. The second introduces the heroine, Flora de Barral. We know nothing of her earlier history, but see Marlow surprising her in a suicide attempt. The next we know of her (at the end of chapter II) is that she has eloped with Captain Anthony. What has happened between the attempted suicide and the elopement we do not know. We are kept in ignorance a further four chapters, during most of which time we are informed of Flora's early life. Then, in the seventh and final chapter of the first section, we are told much more about the elopement. It is this revelation which I propose briefly to examine.

The chapter begins with Marlow and Fyne on the way to London in pursuit of the couple (196). Fyne talks distastefully of the letter Flora left behind—a letter the reader never sees for himself. Fyne goes into the hotel to remonstrate with Captain Anthony. While this meeting is in progress, Marlow accidentally meets Flora in the street.

Conrad gives us in the first place what we may term the present tense of the scene. Marlow is standing on the pavement talking to Flora. Around them bustle the heavy carts and great vans which typify the self-centred impersonality of the great city, concrete details which Conrad has seized on as contrasts to the small, desperately unhappy world of Flora's private life. The girl is well described in details which link her present with her earlier life—her modest, slightly shabby dress, for example, was a gift from Mrs. Fyne.

The reader stands alongside Marlow and sees the scene through his consciousness. Looking at Flora, he wonders what led her to elope with the Captain and reflects on the oddity of the situation in which she can talk of 'the most intimate and final of subjects', death, to a relative stranger (209). As Flora and Marlow talk, people hurry by, among them 'three abominable, drink-sodden loafers' (230). They emphasise the girl's loneliness, her need of help that she will not readily find in such surroundings.

But the reader is not only on the London pavement with Flora; he is also with her during the earlier time of which she is talking, the time of her attempted suicide and subsequent elopement. Both these scenes of past history are brought vividly before us. As we re-experience the first from her point of view, we realise that Marlow's idea that his shout had stopped Flora from throwing herself over the cliff (chapter II) was wrong. The truth was that the Fynes' infernal dog would not leave her and she feared that it might spring over the cliff after her, or, with her gone, sit 'on the brink howling for hours' (203). As it turned out this is a misunderstanding too, a further mockery of her desperation, since Marlow had no sooner appeared than the apparently affectionate dog scampered off.

As he moves from this first to his second scene from Flora's past (the evening before the elopement), Conrad finds himself in difficulties. He has just told us what we need to know of Marlow's first meeting with Flora; he must now tell us of a scene at which Marlow was not present. In doing so he gives Marlow an insight into Flora's mind which we can credit only with difficulty; and in the two paragraphs describing Flora's memories of her father and her 'immense anguish', he writes from the point of view of the omniscient author which he usually took so much trouble to avoid (228–9).

There is yet a further difficulty. We are not really in a London street at all. Marlow is telling his tale in a riverside inn. He is remembering from a fairly distant past the scene that day outside the hotel, just as when he in truth stood there, he was learning from Flora the details of scenes from earlier times still. We think of all three times simultaneously and Conrad is at great pains to make sure that we do.

There are several advantages in this. We have Flora's point of view. We have Marlow's, both at the time the events occurred and later as he looks back and invests a receding past with order and meaning. It is his intelligence that, as so often, prevents sentimentality; it does so by offering many angles from which to judge the affair. There are several disadvantages. The worst is the sense of strain imposed by the three layers of time. It shows itself in Marlow's tedious generalisations, e.g. 'it is a fact that in every man (not in every woman) there lives a lover' (217); and in a typical Conrad unwillingness to commit himself e.g. '. . . I will tell you my idea: my idea is that she went as far as she was able—as far as she could bear it—as far as she had to . . .' (253). This leaves things hanging in the air; it is a kind of riddle.

This was basically the complaint that Henry James made of *Chance* in his essay 'Some Modern Novelists'. The technique, he admitted, was splendid. But what was it all for, except to show its own skill? Of course, he was writing of the complete novel, the second half of which is poorly done—it is difficult to believe in Anthony's behaviour in not sleeping with his wife, and the husband-father relationship is a teased-out business which the reader has to take on trust, there is so little evidence for it.

But in Conrad's favour we must remember one thing. The serious artist will not repeat earlier successes. He will try out new techniques, even though to do so involves risk. *Chance* can be looked on as the furthest limit to which Conrad pushed his experimentation in the handling of time and of different narrators. A writer dedicated to exploring an art form is no less great if alongside his comparative failures such as *Chance* he produces such masterpieces as *Nostromo* and *The Secret Agent*.

8

Technique 3:
Impressionism — Making the Reader
Hear and See

All this experimentation is the result of Conrad's wish to record life accurately. The fluid form of his novels reflects the endless diversity of man's consciousness. Ford claimed that Conrad was an impressionist. In this he was only bearing out Conrad's own statement in the Preface to *The Nigger of the Narcissus*—'my task is to make you hear, to make you feel . . . to make you see; to show a moment of life in its vibration, its colour, its form', and so reveal 'its stress and passion'.

This is a matter of using words, and the words in a novel are either spoken exchanges between the characters, or descriptive or narrative prose.

THE HANDLING OF THE DIALOGUE

Many novelists, Conrad among them, have tried their hands at writing plays. This is a natural result of the importance in fiction of dialogue. All serious novelists use it for a large number of purposes—to reveal and differentiate character and motive, to slacken or quicken the action, to provide contrast or humour, or to pin-point a moment.

Conrad's dialogue is vigorously idiomatic. It is characterised by question and exclamation marks, by 'eh's' and 'By Joves'. He often speaks directly to his reader in the same tone. Here is an example from the start of *Victory*:

> On most evenings of the year Heyst could have sat outside with a naked candle to read one of the books left him by his late father. It was not a mean store. But he never did that. Afraid of mosquitoes, very likely. Neither was he ever tempted by the silence to address any casual remarks to the companion glow of the volcano. He was not mad. Queer chap—yes, that may have been said, and in fact was said; but there is a tremendous difference between the two, you will allow. 4

The clipped, verbless sentences and the appeal at the end ('you will allow') seems to involve the reader in an exchange of views. This is particularly so because Conrad has established a 'tremendous difference' between madness and queerness. By not defining either extreme, he indicates the extent of the area to be explored without committing himself to any definite position.

It is this suggestion of conflicting points of view which gives much of Conrad's prose its typical movement. It also explains the need of a narrator such as Marlow—in speaking directly to his audience of one-time sailors (they are now director of companies, accountant, lawyer) he uses the forceful and idiomatic expressions of ordinary conversation. The first word Conrad makes Marlow speak is 'Yes' as though in reply to someone else; his second sentence begins 'You fellows know . . .' They, and we who read, are thus all implicated in *Youth* from the start.

The vigorous give and take of this kind of prose is a necessary contrast to the mannered Conrad exoticism which has often been anthologised. Part of a paragraph in *Freya of the Seven Isles* runs:

> The brig's business was on uncivilised coasts, with obscure rajahs dwelling in nearly unknown bays; with native settlements up mysterious rivers opening their sombre, forest-lined estuaries among a welter of pale green reefs and dazzling sandbanks, in lonely straits of calm blue water all aglitter with sunshine. Alone, far from the beaten tracks, she glided, all white, round dark, frowning headlands, stole out, like a silent ghost, from behind points of land stretching out all black in the moonlight; or lay hove-to, like a sleeping sea-bird, under the shadow of some nameless mountain waiting for a signal. 171

This has a carefully contrived glamour. The wealth of adjectives and the studied rhythmic control begin to pall. Then suddenly, Conrad brings the reader to earth with briefly spoken words. The natives exclaim: 'Oh, here's a yacht', only to be answered contemptuously by the Dutch captain: 'Yacht! No! That's only English Jasper. A pedlar . . .' (171). It is Conrad's way of taking his reader back to the matter-of-fact world which he so often places side by side with the romantic and fabular.

His characters move in both worlds. Their larger-than-life aspects are expressed in descriptive prose, but their actions in dialogue, as with Jewel in *Lord Jim*. When we first meet her (chapter XXVIII), she is already living with Jim as his wife—that is, we are given an impression, not an explanation or history of her. But there must be some account of her past. Conrad provides it in chapter XXX. In the long opening paragraph, Marlow says that that 'mean and cowardly scoundrel', Cornelius, misused her:

> 'he insisted upon her calling him father—"and with respect too
> —with respect", he would scream, shaking a little yellow fist
> in her face. "I am a respectable man, and what are you? Tell
> me . . ." '   288

This short extract shows Conrad moving within one sentence from description of the past ('he insisted upon . . .') to presentation of a moment of it in the words and gestures of Cornelius. The method is repeated a little later in the same paragraph when we learn of what may be termed Jim's courtship. Moved by Jewel's distress, he 'lounges up' to her to stammer, 'Now—come—really—what's the use—you must try to eat a bite'. Once he says: 'I can stop this game. Just say the word' (289). These broken bits of conversation are very effective, much more so than the typical comments of Marlow—'the endlessness of such a subtly cruel situation was appalling—if you think of it', etc. There are, it is true, some visual details, and we can admire Conrad's precision in using the word 'lounges' of Jim's first self-conscious but sympathetic approach to the girl; but chiefly it is the sound that fixes the scene in our minds. Jim can at first only jerk out exclamations; growing more practical he urges 'eating a bite'; then asserts himself in sharper accents—'Just say the word'. And we accept the fact that he is hers to command, persuaded by these short dramatised moments in Marlow's monologue, even though Jewel herself is silent. We have learned of her through the words of Cornelius and Jim.

At first glance we may be surprised at the apparent casualness of many of the isolated remarks which Conrad gives his characters. The first spoken words in *Typhoon* are Jukes's: 'Allow me, sir', as he expertly rolls the Captain's umbrella (4). They suggest the chief mate's deference, his concern for the ship and its captain, and the general orderliness which is to be a central idea of the tale. That MacWhirr merely mumbles a reply, without looking up, makes its point too. He is fundamentally a lonely man, whose fondness for his 'blessed gamp' is an expression of his routine unimaginative approach to life. It is curious that Conrad even emphasises his extreme taciturnity by an amusing episode which is dependent for its effect on a snatch of dialogue. MacWhirr hears the noise of conversation and asks Jukes: 'Was that you talking just now in the port alleyway?' 'Yes, sir'. At which the Captain goes off to sit on his stool for half an hour, the only sound escaping from him during that time being a sneeze. Then he strolls across to the chief mate to say: 'I can't understand what you find to talk about. Two solid hours . . .' (17–18).

It is a method of revealing character which enables Conrad to involve the reader more closely in the action of his novels. A simple instance can be given from *Falk*. The story is told in the first person by one of a group with whom the reader at least partly identifies himself. A moment comes for revealing that Falk has eaten a man in order to keep alive. Falk and the teller of the tale are talking together, and it is the latter who announces, as though the reader has discovered the truth for himself, 'The carpenter was eaten, of course' (234).

Or, again, the reader can be involved by a character's words being set alongside his thoughts. This is what happens at the start of *Under Western Eyes*, as Razumov struggles to resolve the tensions caused in him by Haldin's sudden appearance. He has to say things to Haldin that are reassuring—the remarks anyone in serious trouble would expect from a friend. But his mind is busy with the effect of this encounter on his future, and as the reader contrasts his thoughts with his actual words, he is taken straight to the heart of the moral issues involved (14 ff.).

The moral issues at the heart of all Conrad's best work are, in fact, usually most clearly revealed in dialogue. *The End of the Tether* (1902) provides a clear instance of this. Its central figure is Captain Whalley, who compromises his integrity for the sake of his undeserving daughter. He conceals the fact of his rapidly worsening blindness. The deception is seen through by Massy, the owner of the ship which Captain Whalley commands; he interferes with the compass and wrecks the vessel for the insurance money.

It is a story with many points of likeness to the first part of *Lord Jim*: both show a good man's honour undermined, both are too long drawn-out. The impressive parts of *The End of the Tether* are the spoken exchanges—between Sterne (the engineer) and Massy in section XI, between Van Wyk and Captain Whalley in section XIII, and between the Captain and Massy in sections VIII and XIV. At these points it is the dialogue which brings fully before the reader the moral implications of the whole action. The climax, too, is in dialogue (329–33), as is the short epilogue which considers why the Captain went down with his ship.

The Secret Sharer (1910) is similarly constructed. An adaptation of a true event, it is the story of a mate who kills an undisciplined member of his crew at a time when the ship's safety demands united action. He is arrested by his captain but escapes by swimming to another ship, which is captained by the narrator of the story. This captain (the 'I' of the story) shelters and saves the mate, in whom he recognises his 'Second Self'—words once considered by Conrad as a title for the story. Their long and excitingly interrupted exchanges explore the mysteries of the tensions within people which pull them in different directions. (Some writers, e.g. Douglas Hewit most persuasively in the opening pages of his *Joseph Conrad: A Reassessment,* read a specially symbolic significance into this story.)

Dialogue is one of Conrad's greatest strengths. He was not capable of the 42nd chapter of Henry James's *Portrait of a Lady,* in which Isabel Archer, alone in a room of her splendid Roman home, brings herself by pursuing a long train of thought to face the truth about the character of Osmond, her husband. But he could have done better than the later still-life scene in which she and the dying Ralph review the past (chapter 54). Less impressive than James with interior monologue, Conrad could be more impressive with dialogue.

His best scenes convey vividly the sense of people thinking of the past, planning for the future, influencing others and revealing in what they say the complexity of human motives and emotions. We think of Nostromo and Decoud out in the dark gulf, of Stevie and his mother making their cab ride across London (*The Secret Agent*), and of Marlow reporting Mistah Kurtz's death in the *Heart of Darkness.* In these great scenes, Conrad selects the spoken words in such a way that the light of moral enquiry plays backwards and forwards through the story, without impairing our belief in the reality of the scene. We are intensely with Nostromo and Decoud in their attempt to save the silver; we follow with equal intensity their exchanges about the 'deadly disease' which the treasure has become.

The interview between Nostromo and Dr. Monygham in the eighth and ninth chapters of 'The Lighthouse' section of the novel is equally impressive (424 ff.). It could well be accorded much closer analysis than there is room for here. Each man has been deeply involved in the fight to save the silver, and the tense words dramatise vividly a crucial moment in the tale. As the two men move from astonishment (the doctor had thought Nostromo dead), through misunderstanding (each obsessed with his own problem and in part using words to disguise his thoughts), to agreed plan of action, we have the sense of all Costaguana spread out before us. The late Señor Hirsch's body dangling from a beam deepens the sense of doom, and Conrad interrupts the interview to describe his death. After this, the men's simplest words take on harsh ironic meanings. At last, Nostromo has been found wanting. He is, he says bitterly of himself, 'nothing to anyone'. 'You do not understand', the doctor tells him. 'I understand you all!', he counters with violence (454). And as he has been brought by these probing, savage exchanges to a moment of insight, so has the reader.

WEAKNESSES

Conrad is an uneven writer. At his best he gives his characters a clearly individual tone—Captain Mitchell is fussy and pompous in speech, Dr. Monygham suspicious and truculent, Giorgio slow and dignified, Nostromo vigorous and practical, Decoud mocking and sophisticated. But Conrad is not always so successful.

He finds it difficult to give Lena in *Victory* the right words and rhythms. We first hear her when Heyst addresses her during the break in the music provided by the Zangiacomo orchestra (near the start of part II). 'I am sure she pinched your arm most cruelly', he says. She replies:

> 'It wouldn't have been the first time. And suppose she did— what are you going to do about it?' 73

A little later he asks if she sings in addition to playing the violin. 'Never sang a note in my life', comes the answer. The tone is forceful; its abruptness suggests vigorous action. But Lena is not at all like that. When she has a long exchange with Heyst after their flight to the island (the beginning of part III), she uses languorous, falling rhythms:

> 'Too big?' he enquired.
> 'Too lonely. It makes my heart sink, too.' 190

The mood is different, it may be argued. True, but it is her normal mood, and the first words remain oddly misleading, more suited to Mrs. Veloc in *The Secret Agent* than to Lena.

The point partly explains Conrad's weakness in depicting women: in giving them a largely passive role he is unable to find the right tone for their speaking voices. Laconic command ('Shop, Adolf. You go.') and scandalised astonishment ('Whatever did you want to do that for?') are exactly right for the purposeful Mrs. Verloc. Conrad matches her decision of character with the terse decisive dialogue that always came easily to him. When he gives the same tone to the very different Lena, the result is unsatisfactory.

Conrad may have been aware of this danger, for many of his heroines speak relatively little. Jewel, in Lord Jim's absence (chapter XXXIX), makes a 'warlike impassioned speech'. It is accorded two lines of text, introduced by Marlow's 'I am told that . . .' (362). For the rest of the book, apart from her despairing outcries at the end, she flits wraith-like in and out of the edges of the reader's consciousness. 'I need not tell you what she is to me', Jim says to Marlow. 'You've seen' (335). Marlow may have seen, but the reader has not. Or, more correctly, he has not heard her, and therefore has to take her on trust.

Those of Conrad's novels which have little or poor dialogue are his weakest. In the main, they are the later works, most obviously *The Arrow of Gold* and *Suspense,* the unfinished last novel. *The Rescue* shows the good and bad side by side. Lingard's yacht, we are told, 'was always precious' to him—like 'old love' (10). This kind of thing (and there is plenty of it) is little more than a vague effusion. When, at a comparable moment, the hero of *The Shadow Line* sees and at once loves the vessel which is to be his first command, he is spoken to by his pilot and by the sneering skipper of the steamship—'I hope you are satisfied with her, Captain' (49)—words which have the effectiveness of those parts of *The Rescue* which leave the dialogue to make its own point. These are the first section of part V and the novel's final pages where Lingard's last instruction ('Steer North') embodies his decision to leave Mr. Travers irrevocably.

In the last resort, of course, Conrad's (or any other writer's) novels are words arranged on a page, and it is in an examination of the skill of the arrangement that the work is to be finally judged. When Conrad took up *The Rescue* again he asked himself what had caused him to abandon it. The suggestions in his Author's Note include the following:

> But I suspect that all the trouble was, in reality, the doubt of my prose, the doubt of its adequacy, of its power to master both the colours and the shades.   ix

So important to any novelist is his control over his words.

IMAGE

We all often have pictures in our minds. Psychologists tell us that these pictures are more than visual. They involve all the senses.

Jung evolved a theory in explanation of the power which images in pictures have over men. A simplified account of the theory may be found in F. Fordham's *An Introduction to Jung's Psychology*; and a fascinating application of the theory to literature in Maud Bodkin's *Archetypal Patterns in Poetry*.

Novelists have always known the importance in their art of the vivid scene. They have brought into being the geography, the society, and the individual men and women of their created worlds; and have often given to one moment of that world's history a brilliance of description which stays with the reader long after the plot, and even the characters' names, have been forgotten. In *Great Expectations* there is the churchyard meeting of young Pip and the convict Magwitch; in *Henry Esmond*, Beatrice, glittering with jewels, coming down the stairs; in *Women in Love*, Birkin stoning the image of the moon reflected in the placid water of the lake.

As an example of one of Conrad's memorable scenes we may take the end of *Victory*. The story has reached its climax.

Heyst has gone out to settle matters with Gentleman Jones. He has given Lena instructions to wait for him at the end of the forest until he gives the sign for her to return to the bungalow. As he and Jones talk, a thunderstorm breaks out. Heyst reveals what Jones did not know: that he has Lena on the island. His initial disgust over, Jones enquires about Lena:

'I have placed her in safety', said Heyst. 'I took good care of that.'

Mr. Jones laid a hand on his arm.

'You have? Look! Is that what you mean?'

Heyst raised his head. In the flicker of lightning the desolation of the cleared ground on his left leaped out and sank into the night, together with the elusive forms of things distant, pale, unearthly. But in the brilliant square of the door he saw the girl—the woman he had longed to see once more—as if enthroned, with her hands on the arms of the chair. She was in black; her face was white, her head dreamily inclined on her breast. He saw her only as low as her knees. He saw her—there, in the room, alive with a sombre reality. It was no mocking vision. She was not in the forest—but there! She sat there in the chair, seemingly without strength, yet without fear, tenderly stooping.

This is one of those scenes that the reader remembers after he has forgotten the story. In Henry James's language, it is 'dramatised'. Conrad synchronises three movements—the lightning, the hand laid on the arm, and the raised head. The lurid effect of lightning is caught in the verbs 'leaped' and 'sank', the movement of which is stilled by the adjectives 'elusive, distant, pale and unearthly'. These prepare us for the framed, motionless picture that follows. Conrad invests it with the formality surrounding royalty—Lena is 'enthroned', her black dress contrasting with her white face. The shock of this image is conveyed to the reader a second time through Heyst's thoughts ('He saw her . . . she was not in the forest—but there!'). The scene has the intensity of a vivid dream, the full force of which ebbs with the falling rhythm of the last longer sentence.

Conrad's novels abound in such scenes. Among the most powerful are the section in *Nostromo* where Decoud and Nostromo take the silver out onto the dark gulf, and the sea-fight which comes at the end of *The Rover*. Conrad presumably wrote them out of an awareness that they had a special significance in their contexts. The scene from *Victory*, quoted above, is the climax of the whole story: Lena is about to gain her 'victory' by sacrificing her life for Heyst's safety. It exemplifies a recurring, historical and artistic situation of the kind Jung called 'archetypal', and it echoes St. Matthew's treatment of the crucifixion. Artists speak for generations of men when they invest such moments with an illumination so vivid as to make them seem timeless.

Conrad's characters often act as a result of a vivid visual impression. As an example we may consider this extract from *Lord Jim*. Jim has jumped from the 'Patna' and is in the little boat with the despicable officers.

> 'If you remember, the ship had been stopped, and was lying with her head on the course steered through the night, with her stern canted high and her bows brought low down in the water through the filling of the fore-compartment. Being thus out of trim, when the squall struck her a little on the quarter, she swung head to wind as sharply as though she had been at anchor. By this change in her position all her lights were in a very few moments shut off from the boat to leeward. It may very well be that, had they been seen, they would have had the effect of a mute appeal—that their glimmer lost in the darkness of the cloud would have had the mysterious power of the human glance that can awaken the feelings of remorse and pity. It would have said, "I am here— still here" . . . and what more can the eye of the most forsaken of human beings say? But she turned her back on them as if in disdain of their fate: she had swung round, burdened, to glare stubbornly at the new danger of the open sea which she so strangely survived to end her days in a breaking-up yard, as if it had been her recorded fate to die obscurely under the blows of many hammers.' 136

The speaker of these words is Marlow. He is commenting on Jim's claim that if he could have seen the 'Patna' he would have swum back to it. Conrad has already emphasised the darkness into which Jim jumped. Now he makes Marlow call up again an impression of the blackness covering the small boat and the larger 'Patna'. Having done this, he gives the 'Patna' human attributes—her lights might have made a mute appeal, almost like an imploring speech; as it is, she 'glares stubbornly' at the open sea and her future fate. This is well done. It suggests that

Jim was driven to jump by the enveloping darkness, by his imagination and not by his reason; and it suggests to the reader a comparison between the irresolute, even cowardly Jim and the stoical ship 'glaring stubbornly'. Conrad is commenting on Jim's action in images which speak for themselves. He advances both his story and its meaning by means of them.

I shall consider as a third and final example of the power of Conrad's set scenes the start of *Under Western Eyes*. The introduction to the narrator over, there is a dramatic account of the murder and of the murderer's (Haldin's) retreat to student Razumov's room. Razumov goes to arrange for Haldin's escape that night, finds the owner of the sledge drunk, beats him with 'an insatiable fury, in great volleys of sounding thwacks' (30), and then walks off into the snow-covered streets, uncertain what to do. There is much in the conduct of these thirty pages to admire, but the paragraphs I wish to consider are these:

> Suddenly on the snow, stretched on his back right across his path, he saw Haldin, solid, distinct, real, with his inverted hands over his eyes, clad in brown close-fitting coat and long boots. He was lying out of the way a little, as though he had selected that place on purpose. The snow round him was untrodden.
>
> This hallucination had such a solidity of aspect that the first movement of Razumov was to reach for his pocket to assure himself that the key of his room was there. But he checked the impulse with a disdainful curve of his lips. He understood. His thought, concentrated intensely on the figure left lying on his bed, had culminated in this extraordinary illusion of the sight. Razumov tackled the phenomenon calmly. With a stern face, without a check and gazing far beyond the vision, he walked on, experiencing nothing but a slight tightening of the chest. After passing he turned his head for a glance, and saw only the unbroken track of his footsteps over the place where the breast of the phantom had been lying. Razumov walked on and after a little time whispered his wonder to himself.
>
> 'Exactly as if alive! seemed to breathe! and right in my way too! I have had an extraordinary experience.' He made a few steps and muttered through his teeth—'I shall give him up.'

36–7

There are three stages here. First, Conrad gives us the vivid details of what Razumov sees. They are made more exciting by the dramatically broken rhythm of the short phrases and single words. The untrodden snow forms the climax of this section—how has the body got there, placed to one side of Razumov's path, if the snow around it is smooth? Perhaps Haldin is real, after all. We get a strong impression that Razumov wishes he were.

But the second stage, beginning with the word 'hallucinattion', dispels this idea. Haldin may look so solid, distinct and real that Razumov has to reassure himself by feeling for his keys, but he cannot really be there—he is locked in Razumov's room. The two contradictory states are placed harshly side by side and Razumov struggles to master his fear. The reference to his disdain and the assured finality of the words 'he understood' convey superbly the intellectual confidence of a young student dealing with a problem he intends to master. This paragraph, too, has its climax, reached when Razumov successfully wills himself to walk over the 'body'. A backward glance shows that the smooth snow has been broken only by his own footsteps.

A lesser writer might well have left the scene there. But Conrad is moving towards the crucial moment from which all later events will stem. He allows Razumov to walk on, and to 'whisper his wonder to himself'—well-chosen words with a sinister sound. It is sound not sight that now chiefly moves us as we enter the movement of Razumov's mind. Still struggling to make sense of what has happened, he formulates a confident idea whose over-simplification is ultimately seen as grimly ironic —'I have had an extraordinary experience'. Then with grim determination and apparently total irrationality he announces, 'I shall give him up'.

This is great writing. Its economy of visual detail, matched by taut phrasing, culminates in the spoken word as Razumov's excited and incomplete sentences lead to his clear pronouncement to give Haldin up. It is in no way a logical decision. Yet so compulsive has it been made to seem that we accept it as the inevitable result of the illusion. We are more than observers of

Razumov; we have identified ourselves with him. At such an important moment of the novel this is a triumph of technique. The betrayal which is to determine Razumov's whole future cannot at any time be forgotten by the reader, who will without warning come against reminders of Haldin's body stretched out on the whiteness of the snow. It was an obstacle in Razumov's path. It will continue to be an obstacle to his peace of mind until he at last confesses to the dead man's sister.

SYMBOL

Do these scenes have a further, deeper meaning behind the concrete world they present? Are they, to put it another way, symbolic? Perhaps the best way to answer the question is to give another example.

It comes from the second page of *Almayer's Folly*. In the opening three paragraphs Almayer has been dreaming of the future, and imagining himself, wealthy and respected, living with his daughter in Europe, far away from his present surroundings. The swollen river by which he stands is carrying driftwood past him.

> One of those drifting trees grounded on the shelving shore, just by the house, and Almayer, neglecting his dream, watched it with languid interest. The tree swung slowly round, amid the hiss and foam of the water, and soon getting free of the obstruction began to move downstream again, rolling slowly over, raising upwards a long, denuded branch, like a hand lifted in mute appeal to heaven against the river's brutal and unnecessary violence. Almayer's interest in the fate of that tree increased rapidly. He leaned over to see if it would clear the low point below. It did; then he drew back, thinking that now its course was free down to the sea, and he envied the lot of that inanimate thing now growing small and indistinct in the deepening darkness. As he lost sight of it altogether he began to wonder how far out to sea it would drift. Would the current carry it north or south? South, probably, till it drifted in sight of Celebes, as far as Macassar, perhaps! 4

If we wish to think of this paragraph symbolically, we may analyse it as follows—the drifting log transfers our thoughts to Almayer himself, a man without direction and at the mercy of event; the 'brutal violence' of the river suggests that life has dealt him some hard blows; and the glimpse of the log's future course becomes Almayer's ultimate fate, at present hidden from us. There cannot be much doubt that Conrad intended something of this because he shows us the floating tree through Almayer's eyes. Almayer, we are told, 'envied the lot of that inanimate thing', and this implies a comparison between them.

If we now return to *Under Western Eyes*, and the imaginary body lying in the snow, we find an immediate likeness to the scene in *Almayer's Folly*: description and thought are closely interwoven. Razumov, like Almayer, is interpreting to himself the meaning of what he sees (or thinks he sees) about him. This being so, there is really no question of symbol or deeper meaning. We are simply sharing Razumov's life and thought.

Still, Razumov's hallucination does come to take on a special significance for him and therefore for the reader. Haldin's body blocked his way when he originally saw it and was the immediate cause of the betrayal. After this, Razumov is never again at peace with himself. In betraying Haldin he has unwittingly betrayed his own honour, and it is his memory of the body, still lying in the way, that remains inescapably with him as a vivid reminder of his guilt. And this is no doubt one way in which in real life we are brought face to face with moral issues—by visual memory. In the case of Razumov, there is another interesting aspect of his obsession with the dead Haldin. Whether or not Conrad intended it, the fact that Razumov imagined what was not in truth there suggests that his subsequent betrayal was the act of a deluded mind; he was, as we say, not himself. Only confession can restore his wholeness.

After he has purged his fault, a heavy shower passes over him as he walks home. This time there can be no doubt of Conrad's intentions, since Razumov meets his landlord who, 'just to say something', observes 'You've got very wet'. 'Yes', mutters Razumov, 'I am washed clean' (357). The admission is not commented on by either Razumov himself or by Conrad as author, and it is from this restraint that it gains its force. To the landlord who is only indulging in small talk, it remains meaningless.

Symbolism of this kind has its dangers. They are seen in Razumov's confession to Miss Haldin (347–56). At the time, Miss Haldin is wearing a veil which falls to the floor. Razumov picks it up, presses it to his face and carries it away with him. This action, and indeed the whole business with the veil, is clearly meant to symbolise something—presumably the fact that the barrier between Razumov and Miss Haldin is at last being broken down. But the reader is in the main only vaguely and uneasily aware that the veil ought to have special significance; he is not clear what that significance is. And, as usually happens, Conrad's prose betrays his uncertainty of touch; it is over-dramatic and portentous.

Some novelists create their worlds and are content to leave them to their readers for the discernment of meaning. Defoe does this. Even if there is conscious irony in, say, *Moll Flanders*, there is also much of the recording camera. Others, of whom Conrad is one, suggest for their created worlds metaphorical applications to life as a whole. An extreme example is Herman Melville, whose *Moby Dick* has something of the appeal of myth, suggesting a larger meaning than that contained in the lives of the characters. If, however, we say that the great white whale is fate or some similar force against which Ahab cannot help rebelling, we deal with only one aspect of the novel, and that perhaps misleadingly. We need always to do more than search out 'the meaning' of a novel or of any work of art; we need to consider fully and in context the words and actions of all the characters if we are to experience the whole.

In the sense that Conrad deliberately presents his stories as though they have applications beyond their own confines, it is useful to think of him as a writer who uses images symbolically. The whole of *The Nigger of the Narcissus* and *The Secret Sharer* can be thought of in this way. It is a method of writing which has its dangers, particularly if it is resorted to often or is allowed to get in the way of the plain story. But at its best it can be very powerful.

Here is Nostromo's awakening on the morning after he has stolen the silver:

> He lay as if dead. A rey-zamuro, appearing like a tiny black speck in the blue, stooped, circling prudently with a stealthiness of flight startling in a bird of that great size. The shadow of his pearly-white body, of his black-tipped wings, fell on the grass no more silently than he alighted himself on a hillock of rubbish within three yards of that man, lying as still as a corpse. The bird stretched his bare neck, craned his bald head, loathsome in the brilliance of varied colouring, with an air of voracious anxiety towards the promising stillness of that prostrate body. Then, sinking his head deeply into his soft plumage, he settled himself to wait. The first thing upon which Nostromo's eyes fell on waking was this patient watcher for the signs of death and corruption. When the man got up the vulture hopped away in great sidelong, fluttering jumps. He lingered for a while, morose and reluctant, before he rose, circling noiselessly with a sinister droop of beak and claw.
>
> Long after he had vanished, Nostromo, lifting his eyes up to the sky, muttered, 'I am not dead yet'.   413

There is a Graham Greene repulsion about the bird—the vultures at the start of both *The Heart of the Matter* and *The Power and the Glory* have the same effect on the reader. Its patient waiting for Nostromo's corruption anticipates a process already begun by the theft. Its noiseless arrival and departure suggest the scarcely noticeable inevitability of Nostromo's future moral deterioration. Physically, he is 'not dead yet'; morally he is. Moments like this are one mark of Conrad's greatness.

9

Attitude to the Imagination

Conrad's main themes and their development are fairly clear. In the early Malayan novels, the sweep of the earth, sea and sky and the exotic profusion of the tropics form the background against which men act out their lives. It is an unfriendly background.

> Out of the level blue of a shallow sea Carimata raises a lofty barrenness of grey and yellow tints, the drab eminence of its arid heights. Separated by a narrow strip of water, Suroeton, to the West, shows a curved and ridged outline resembling the backbone of a stooping giant. And to the eastward a troop of insignificant islets stand effaced, indistinct, with vague features that seem to melt into the gathering shadows. The night following from the eastward retreat of the setting sun advanced slowly, swallowing the land and the sea; the land broken, tormented and abrupt; the sea smooth and inviting with its easy polish of continuous surface to wanderings facile and endless.   5

This is from the opening pages of *The Rescue*. It describes darkness falling on an uninhabited and sinister landscape. The jagged heights have human attributes (they are giant-like, tormented and broken), and the insidiously polished surface of the sea snares men into meaningless wanderings. It is a continuation of the manner of *Almayer*, where the luxuriant jungle mocks his bitter fate; it carries over into the later works: the forbidding precipices of the Azuera (*Nostromo*) and the hard Russian winter (*Under Western Eyes*) are at best indifferent, at worst hostile.

In such circumstances men protect themselves as well as they can. As far as a ship's crew are concerned, their safety depends on combined action. The crew of the 'Narcissus', as we have seen, found its salvation by disciplined seamanship during a great storm. For Conrad, it was the same on land. Men were still threatened, even if by enemies less obvious than the menace of sea and wind. He saw organised society as an expression of men's attempt at self-defence against the hostility of their surroundings.

There is clear expression of the idea at the start of *An Outpost of Progress*. Two white men, Kayerts and Carlier, have just arrived at an isolated trading station to which they have been assigned. Conrad comments:

> They were two perfectly insignificant and incapable individuals, whose existence is only rendered possible through the high organisation of civilised crowds. Few men realise that their life, the very essence of their character, their capabilities and their audacities, are only the expression of their belief in the safety of their surroundings. The courage, the composure, the confidence; the emotions and principles; every great and every insignificant thought belongs not to the individual but to the crowd: to the crowd that believes blindly in the irresistible force of its institutions and of its morals, in the power of its police and of its opinion. But the contact with pure unmitigated savagery, with primitive nature and primitive man, brings sudden and profound trouble into the heart. To the sentiment of being alone of one's kind, to the clear perception of the loneliness of one's thoughts, of one's sensations—to the negation of the habitual, which is safe, there is added the affirmation of the unusual, which is dangerous; a suggestion of things vague, uncontrollable, and repulsive, whose discomposing intrusion excites the imagination and tries the civilised nerves of the foolish and the wise alike.
>
> 89

The crowd, this paragraph tells us, is what gives man confidence. But the confidence is illusory. It blinds men to the truth of the human situation. That truth Conrad expressed to Cunninghame Graham in 1897 in the following terms:

> Know thyself. Understand that you are nothing, less than a shadow, more insignificant than a drop of water in the ocean, more fleeting than the illusion of a dream.
>
> JOSEPH CONRAD: LIFE AND LETTERS I, 215

Man is not even such stuff as dreams are made on—he is the illusion of a dream. So Conrad places before us men and women who are alone, and who, without the comforting deceptions possible in crowds, find their hearts profoundly troubled. Their struggle to maintain in the face of this realisation their integrity, their basic decency as human beings, forms one of Conrad's main themes.

TEMPTATIONS OF THE IMAGINATION: 'HEART OF DARKNESS'

A. E. Housman said that man was alone and afraid in a world he had not made. The words express neatly the theme which occupied Conrad after *The Nigger of the Narcissus*. Both *Heart of Darkness* (1899) and *Lord Jim* (1900) deal with it.

The first is an account of a journey up the Congo and into the depth of the jungle. It is told by Marlow. Its aim is to suggest the horrifying possibilities of that great part of men's minds 'where doubt itself is lost in an unexplored universe of incertitudes'. Conrad shows how some situations will force men back to uncivilised states where centuries of social and cultural achievement are lost in a great blackness of the mind. According to the Author's Note the events are 'experience pushed a little (and only a very little) beyond the actual facts of the case' (vii).

From the moment Marlow sets foot in Africa he finds all decencies threatened. Even near the coast he finds life sordid, and admires his company's chief accountant who displays backbone by dressing immaculately in order to withstand the demoralisation of his surroundings. Further inland no measures are strong enough to form a barrier against the dense jungle and its orgiastic native life. Kurtz, the company's most successful agent, had at first hoped to bring the light of civilisation into the great darkness of Africa. He even wrote an inspiring memorandum on the problems, having been entrusted by the International Society for the Suppression of Savage Customs with making a report for its future guidance. It is all useless; in the end, he succumbs to the seductions of the jungle, exercising for the most diabolical ends his unrestrained power over the natives. Ultimately he comes to realise what has happened to himself, and at the end of his report scrawls in an unsteady hand the addition: 'Exterminate all the brutes' (118). His last words are a whispered, 'The Horror! The Horror!' (149).

Conrad is determined, however, to make his reader understand that the fate of Kurtz is that of any man placed in the same position. He brings Marlow, too, to the point of mental breakdown:

> 'No, they did not bury me, though there is a period of time which I remember mistily, with a shuddering wonder, like a passage through some inconceivable world that had no hope in it and no desire'.　　　　　　　　152

Back in Europe, he is angered by the ordinary life of the city, whose people cannot possibly know the things he now knows. He then understands better the cryptic enquiries of the doctor who had examined him prior to his departure:

> 'I always ask leave, in the interests of science, to measure the crania of those going out there', the doctor said. 'And when they come back too?' I asked. 'Oh, I never see them', he remarked; 'and, moreover, the changes take place inside, you know. . . . Ever any madness in your family?'　　　58

Heart of Darkness is a story of great power. In spite of its proliferation of adjectives—for Conrad was still learning to let the tale make its own point—it represents a deepening of his art. The laconic and famous, 'Mistah Kurtz—he dead' (150), was used by T. S. Eliot as an epigraph to *The Hollow Men*.

Lord Jim pushes the same theme further. As we have already seen (pp. 78–81), it is an extended study of the state of mind of a man who has succumbed to the equivalent of the unknown terrors of the jungle, without either giving in to his baser self (like Kurtz) or taking refuge in flight (like Marlow who came home ill). Jim is the chief mate on the 'Patna' which is taking a large number of pilgrims to Mecca. The ship strikes a hidden object, springs a leak, and seems likely to sink. The officers, ignoring Jim as they do not consider him one of their kind, plan to leave the passengers to their fate. At the last moment, after watching in stony and almost paralysed disapproval their preparations to desert, Jim jumps into their boat. But the 'Patna' does not sink, is found drifting by a French gunboat, and is towed to safety.

The first half of the novel investigates minutely Jim's action. Marlow, who tells the tale, sympathises with Jim from the moment the two exchange an understanding glance at the official Court of Inquiry. He sees that Jim is too imaginative, that circumstances have worked against him, and that he is very different from his fellow-officers who are merely despicable. Yet Marlow sees, too, that Jim's failure is a moral one, and is in the last resort inexcusable. He knows that Jim, in thinking back about his desertion, is more concerned with the chance he missed of obtaining glory, than with the fate of the wretched pilgrims. He notes grimly that a betrayal of this kind springs from 'subtle unsoundness' of character. In considering the business from many angles, Marlow comments and analyses at great length and with much complication.

Conrad controls his material well. Marlow's choice of words, his hesitations, anecdotes and irrelevancies are made to bear on the problem of Jim's moral lapse. Facts and references are so placed that they can be thought of only in comparison with Jim's disgrace—the Malayans on board the 'Patna' stick faithfully to their routine tasks simply because they received no order to do otherwise; the officer of the French gunboat cannot even begin to understand the desertion of a ship loaded with pas-

sengers—'when the honour is gone . . . I can offer no opinion
. . . because—monsieur—I know nothing of it' (148); and then
there is the case of Bob Stanton who was drowned 'trying to
save a lady's maid in the 'Sophora' disaster' (149). These incidents
are more telling than the Court of Inquiry in showing by
comparison the measure of Jim's shame. At other times Marlow
helps us to think of Jim more sympathetically—we learn of the
sheltered upbringing; of the failure to arise to an occasion when
in training; and of the extraordinary suicide of the Judge who
presided at the Inquiry. There are some good comments on
these things (and especially on the symbolic imagery of the
novel) in Tony Tanner's *Conrad: Lord Jim*.

The trial over, there follows a kind of link section. Jim tries
a number of obscure jobs but leaves each when brought against
reminders of the 'Patna' affair. Then he meets Stein, an older
man whose life has divided itself into two neat halves—man of
action and, later, dreamer and butterfly collector. Even more
than Marlow, he is qualified to understand Jim. He arranges to
send him to Patusan, a country cut off from civilisation by thirty
miles of jungle. With Jim's entry into it we reach the second
half of the novel, where our concern is his effort to atone for
the error which has been the theme so far.

At first, Jim's progress is triumphal. He escapes imprisonment
by leaping over a stockade—a victorious leap this time, the scene
of which he proudly shows Marlow. He fights a successful
battle, gains control over the Rajah, and achieves a dominant
position among Doramin's people. Once again, however, he is
brought into contact with evil men. When the coarse and
unscrupulous adventurer, Brown, comes to Patusan with his
gang, Jim grants him a safe conduct. Taking advantage of this,
Brown makes common cause with Cornelius (the unsavoury
father of Jim's native girl), and murders Doramin's son and his
followers. As Jim had pledged his life against Patusan's safety,
the only course open to him is to let himself be shot by Doramin.

F. R. Leavis (in *The Great Tradition*) has said that the second
half of *Lord Jim*, though impressive, lacks the inevitability of
the first half. This is true. The comments and incidents bearing

on the main theme are still there. The last letter from Jim's father is a good example, with its assertion:

> Virtue is one all over the world, and there is only one faith, one conceivable conduct of life, one manner of dying . . . who once gives way to temptation in the very instant hazards his total depravity and everlasting ruin. 341

But Conrad does not make his point completely clear. Whereas Jim's first fault was a moral error, a mistake brought about by a failure of conscience, his second is different. It is, at least partly, an error of judgment, a mistake brought about by misunderstanding the situation. Yet the second is allied to the first. There are frequent hints that Jim is still 'subtly unsound'. Marlow brutally tells Jim's girl that her lover can never return to the world of civilisation because 'he is not good enough' (318), and Jim seems paralysed by Brown's 'sickening assumption of his and Jim's common guilt'. Brown senses that Jim has no right to 'come the righteous over him' (387).

It is thus not possible to reduce *Lord Jim* to one formula of interpretation applicable to Melville's *Billy Budd*: the eternal victimisation of the good (Billy) by the wicked (Claggart), with the power of authority (Captain Vere) mainly concerned to insist on the legal rules for the sake of order and decency. Billy Budd's fault is naïveté, allied to his unfortunate stammer; Jim's is moral cowardice. *Lord Jim* is rather a statement of the dangers of the imagination. It led Jim astray when he leapt overboard from the 'Patna', and it led him astray again in allowing him to build up his world in Patusan. For Patusan is in its own way an illusion. Unless he had died for his illusion, Jim would not have been worthy of his title of Lord Jim.

The ultimate truth behind the story seems to be that, even if Lord Jim is 'not good enough', then 'nobody is good enough' (319). Another comment by Marlow epitomises the whole novel:

> 'The last word is not said—probably never shall be said. Are not our lives too short for that full utterance which through all our stammerings is of course our only and abiding intention?' 225

At first sight it may seem surprising that *Lord Jim* was followed by *Typhoon*. The earlier novel is long and complicated, the later one short and relatively simple. But in fact Conrad is still dealing with the same theme. Having shown how men of imagination attempt to control their lives, he now depicts a man of no imagination. How does he fare in a hostile world?

It is a subject already touched on in the figure of Singleton in *The Nigger of the Narcissus* (38). Cunninghame Graham suggested to Conrad in 1897 that he should have made Singleton a more educated man. Conrad's reply was unusually emphatic:

> . . . Singleton with an education is impossible. But first of all—what education? If it is the knowledge of how to live, my man essentially possessed it. He was in perfect accord with life. If by education you mean scientific knowledge then the question arises, what knowledge? How much of it—in what direction? Is it to stop at plane trigonometry or at conic sections? Or is he to study Platonism or Pyrrhonism, or the philosophy of the gentle Emerson? Or do you mean the kind of knowledge which would enable him to scheme, and lie, and intrigue his way to the forefront of a crowd no better than himself? Would you seriously, of malice prepense, cultivate in that unconscious man the power to think? Then he would become conscious—and much smaller—and very unhappy. Now he is simple and great like an elemental force. Nothing can touch him but the curse of decay—the eternal decree that will extinguish the sun, the stars, one by one, and in another instant shall spread a frozen darkness over the whole universe. Nothing else can touch him—he does not think.

> JOSEPH CONRAD: LIFE AND LETTERS I, 214–15

Captain MacWhirr of *Typhoon* is similarly untouchable. He is a stoic whose unyielding resistance to all misfortune is the direct result of his unthinking nature. He has 'just enough imagination to carry him through each successive day and no more', and this makes him 'tranquilly sure' of himself (4). His strength is derived from the unruffled ordinariness of which his unrolled but elegant umbrella is a symbol. He cannot understand the mate's suggestion that it might be well to head the ship off her course for a time in an effort to evade the storm. Captain MacWhirr is not the man to evade anything which lies in what he regards as the plain path of duty. Once in the storm, he stares helplessly but determinedly into its blackness, as though steeling his own will to the head-on conflict. Then the Chinamen he is carrying start fighting, and become a seething, uncontrollable mass of arms and legs. The mate is tersely informed, 'Can't have fighting board ship', and is sent to set matters to rights. The Captain reflects that he is glad the—

> trouble in the 'tween deck had been discovered in time. If the ship had to go after all, then, at least, she wouldn't be going to the bottom with a lot of people in her fighting teeth and claw. That would have been odious.   85

The hurricane, as it were, finds a stoic in its path, but does no more than wring from him the words, uttered in a tone of vexation: 'I shouldn't like to lose her' (86). Nor does he; and it is his sense of the fitness of things that leads him, once the storm is over and the Chinese are restored to order, to work out a plan for dealing with the money which had caused all the trouble by rolling out of the chests at the height of the storm. The mate wants to pass the responsibility on to someone else when the ship reaches port, and even brings rifles for fear of further disorder. But the captain insists on sharing the money out equally, and the three dollars left over he gives to the three most damaged coolies. As the chief mate remarks to close the book: 'I think he got out of it very well for such a stupid man' (102).

Typhoon is a minor masterpiece. It is a vivid account of life on board ship during a storm and is economically unified around the theme of the Captain's stubborn heroism. He does indeed 'get out of it' well. But his is not an attitude which forms a subject of Conrad's later work. In the larger, more modern world of Costaguana (where we have moved into the twentieth century), instead of MacWhirr we have old Giorgio, the unquestioning supporter of Garibaldi. His integrity and courage are beyond doubt, but he is the relic of an earlier century and stands uncomprehendingly on the side-lines while the great affairs of the mine are acted out around him. And in other novels, the Captain's stoicism has developed into the fanatical service of a fixed idea. Mrs. Verloc and Ossipon, Haldin and his revolutionary associates pursue aims as limited as Captain Mac-Whirr's, but they are less worthy aims: dangerous obsessions is a better description of them. Their world is in any case too complicated for the simple virtues which are enough for life on board a sailing vessel. We admire Captain MacWhirr, but we need to look beyond him.

10

Man in Society

Conrad admitted in the Author's Note to *Nostromo* that the period following the publication of the 'Typhoon' volume of stories was a difficult one—'it seemed somehow that there was nothing more in the world to write about' (vii).

In retrospect, the feeling is understandable. Most of the stories up to this time had been about the neatly confined communities of ships' crews or about the moral struggles of one man, but while they were being written, Conrad and Ford were discussing at great length the technical aspects of novel-writing. The discussions must have suggested the need for new themes no less than for new forms.

An aspect of *Lord Jim* suggests that this was so. It was planned in the first place as a short story. Its growth was very likely connected with the explorations of Ford and Conrad which went on during its composition. The result is that the technical complication of *Lord Jim* is too great for the subject, which remains that of a much shorter book. This partly explains Leavis's criticisms of the later scenes in Patusan.

'NOSTROMO'

In *Nostromo* there is no disparity between theme and treatment. While we are concerned with individuals and their moral problems, it is in effect a whole state which is under consideration. Conrad claimed that 'there was not a single brick, stone or grain of sand of Costaguana's soil' that he had not placed in position with his own hands (*A Personal Record*, 100). During the two years of the novel's writing, he felt that he had been on a sojourn to the continent of Latin America. The characters that move against this background are not observed mainly from within, as are Lord Jim and the Marlow of *Heart of Darkness*. They are also seen often from outside (there is no Marlow in *Nostromo*). They pass comments on each other, and the reader is left to judge them and their world for himself.

The action centres round the silver of the San Tomé mine, the continued safety of which is imperilled by a South American revolution. This mine is in several ways the meeting point of the lives of a whole coastal area, and for the first time Conrad's art moves easily through the various political, social, religious, military and purely personal levels. If it is in any way meaningful to speak of the theme of such a long and complicated novel, then *Nostromo* is a statement of the difficulties and dangers which beset men who pursue political and economic ends, however worthy the ends may seem. Martin Decoud is for a time the explicit spokesman for this point of view. Born in Costaguana, though long since sophisticated by living in Paris, he is drawn back to his native land by love of Antonia. He is openly scornful of the obsessions of both political parties. He points out several times that all such worldly interests as are represented by the silver of the mine must of necessity coarsen people. To cultured minds, he says, 'the narrowness of every belief is odious' (187), and, as a newspaper correspondent (an occupation he allows himself to take up in spite of his scepticism), he asserts that 'there is no room for effective truth in politics or journalism' (177). Yet he, too, is drawn into playing his part in events, and the plan to save the silver of the mine is his.

More important, however, than Decoud's utterances are the lives of those involved in running the mine. Without exception, they find their integrity threatened. Those who finance it from a distance are sketched in with a controlled but severe irony—people's lives to them are but part of the furniture needed for their profits; those who are apparently outside its tentacles, like the Garibaldino, the apostle of freedom who lived his significant years during the Italian freedom movement of his youth and who now lives mainly in remembering the great days, become implicated through their families; and those who believe blindly in the importance of the mine and the political régime that its continuance requires, are (like Captain Mitchell) hopelessly duped by events—Captain Mitchell, in fact, is the party spokesman, the official apologist who has in reality no idea what is going on.

This brings us to characters seen in greater detail. There are the Goulds who own the mine. They are both good people. Charles has devoted his life to its service in the belief that it, and it alone, can bring order to Costaguana. He has come to idealise it in his imagination—indeed, the whole novel can be viewed as a study in the 'spiritual value which everyone discovers in his own form of activity' (318). He has thus almost forgotten the early (and necessarily continuing) 'accommodation to existing circumstances of corruption' (142), which was the price of his life's work. His wife, on the other hand, sees the cost plainly; she knows that the mine has destroyed their married life—for though Gould is in a way perfect, she 'would never have him to herself, never, not for one short hour altogether to herself'; and she knows that its very success has 'carried with it the moral degradation of the idea' (521). In one way, both Goulds have been destroyed by the mine: they have paid far too high a price in terms of individual integrity and of married understanding to make the sacrifice worth while.

Then there is Nostromo himself, the man of the people, the 'incorruptible Capataz' who is to save the threatened mine by taking away in a lighter by night the silver which the revolutionists will otherwise capture. The mainspring of his actions is understood by Decoud—'the only thing he seems to care for is to be well spoken of'. He makes an interesting addition to this judgment—'An ambition fit for noble souls, but also a profitable one for an exceptionally intelligent scoundrel' (246). Nostromo is not specially intelligent. In truth, he is romantically naïve (shades of Lord Jim), and when he is brought into closer contact with the mine he is betrayed by it. Until the scene on the gulf, he remains incorruptible. But Decoud's scepticism (he has no choice but to act alongside Decoud) and the blackness of the night undermine his hitherto unwavering confidence. 'Deprived of certain simple realities, such as the admiration of women, the adulation of men, and the admired publicity of his life', he steals the silver. As he shrewdly grows rich little by little, 'he feels the burden of sacrilegious guilt descend upon his shoulders' (420).

There is, of course, a serious danger of distortion in speaking so summarily of so complicated a novel. Still, it is along these lines that the statement of the artistic whole may be understood, for it is fairly well unified round the main themes, though not as much so as *Lord Jim*.

Critics agree that the second half of the novel is a falling-off. After Decoud's death, Nostromo realises that he alone knows where the treasure is hidden; everyone else imagines it at the bottom of the gulf. He therefore makes occasional journeys to its hiding place. A lighthouse is built on the same island, however, and kept by Giorgio Viola and his two daughters, Linda and Giselle. Nostromo goes to steal yet more silver, is mistaken by Viola for a suitor, and is shot.

A new theme appears in this last section. It stems from the earlier obsession with moral failure, but also looks ahead to the novels to come. It is provided by Dr. Monygham, the medical officer of the San Tomé mine, whose sudden prominence at this late stage does not unbalance the novel as much as might be expected, since his doings are contrasted with those of Nostromo. At the start of events, the Doctor is 'withered and shrunk by the shame of moral disgrace' (431), never having recovered from the fictitious confessions forced out of him by an earlier tyrant of Costaguana. It had been necessary for some plot to be unveiled, and there was an inquisitor to hand who excelled at wringing falsehoods from selected victims. But the Doctor later often wondered, 'grinding his teeth with shame and rage, at the fertility of his imagination when stimulated by a sort of pain which makes truth, honour, self-respect, and life itself matters of little moment' (373). Like Lord Jim (and with less reason), he is appalled by the fact that he is, 'in the eyes of respectable people, a man careless of common decencies'; like Lord Jim, he sets about re-establishing his honour, at least in his own eyes.

So, while Nostromo falls from grace, and while even Charles Gould realises bitterly that the impossibility of 'disengaging his activity from its debasing contacts' has by now 'insidiously corrupted his judgment' (364), Dr. Monygham remakes his shattered life by taking heroic risks for the Gould concession. He does so out of high regard for Mrs. Gould, knowing that to save the mine is to save what little may be left of the meaning of her life. The illusion of the mine claims him at last, as it claims the others, though the Doctor's activity is 'exalted by a spiritual detachment from the usual sanctions of hope and reward', and he is motivated by the 'proud feeling that his devotion is the only thing standing between an admirable woman and a frightful disaster' (431). It is this salvation through devotion to a person that is to form the new theme of Conrad's later work.

Conrad described *Nostromo* as a story of 'events flowing from the passions of men short-sighted in good and evil' (ix). It is his most considerable achievement. Except that its concluding section is disappointing, its sweep and power would have made it one of the very finest of English novels.

THE SCEPTICISM OF 'NOSTROMO'

There is in *Nostromo* an acute awareness of the contradictions in human nature. Conrad knew that men often pretend to be what they are not, or deceive themselves about their real motives, or use for their own advantage the gullibility of others. This knowledge found expression in an irony exercised most notably in dealing with men's political and commercial activities. Conrad often treated these with great scorn.

A good instance occurs at the start of the fifth chapter of 'The Lighthouse' section of *Nostromo*. It describes the entry into Sulaco of Pedrito Montero and his revolutionary supporters. This riff-raff now honours itself with the title 'Sulaco National Guard'. The crowd yells 'Vivas', and in order to make them more enthusiastic, Pedrito slips his hands under the arms of the henchman riding next to him—all men are now brothers. In the main plaza he makes a speech. The crowd hears little, but loves the sight of his clenched fist and his arm flung above his head. Occasionally, a few hackneyed phrases like 'the happiness of the people' are audible to most of the mob. His speech finished, Pedrito (by now 'His Excellency') makes way for Gamacho, who urges that war should be declared at once against France, England, Germany and the United States of America (392). Clearly Conrad is at this point in danger of becoming absurd; his satire is running away with him. But it is a momentary lapse and signifies little in so long and complex a book—in any case he regains stricter control of his heavily ironic manner when he later shows the National Guard neglecting its duty and Gamacho snoring in sordid surroundings just when he is needed. Social and political posturings are a favourite butt of Conrad. The conspirators in *Under Western Eyes*, the progressive Fynes and the newspaper men in *Chance*, the Tropical Belt Company in *Victory* and the ministerial world of *The Secret Agent* are all presented to the reader with fierce scorn.

Many of Conrad's characters have little or no ironic sense. They can mock neither their own nor other people's behaviour. If this is a strength, as in Captain MacWhirr (*Typhoon*), Mr. Baker (*The Nigger*) and the French Lieutenant (*Lord Jim*), it is the strength of limitation. More often it is a serious weakness. A greater ability to suspect and cast a cold eye on human pretensions might have saved Almayer and Lord Jim, Nostromo and Miss Haldin from their fates. For irony in the sense in which it is being considered here is much more than an occasional manipulation of words. It is a whole way of looking at life, an ingrained habit of standing apart from the world of action and judging it in the cynical light of one's knowledge of men's inconsistencies and dishonesties.

Now Nostromo has a limited, half-unconscious suspicion of at least some human organisations. This explains his refusal to fetch a priest to the dying Teresa—he 'did not believe in Priests in their sacerdotal character; they were incapable of good or harm' (255). Nevertheless, when he learns of her death, he exclaims, 'May God rest her soul'—an odd expression for one so distrustful of the church. Conrad makes this comment on it:

> Sharing in the anti-priestly freethought of the masses, his [Nostromo's] mind used the pious formula from the superficial force of habit, but with a deep-seated sincerity. The popular mind is incapable of scepticism; and that incapacity delivers their helpless strength to the wiles of swindlers and to the pitiless enthusiasms of leaders inspired by visions of a high destiny.   420

The word 'scepticism' is the interesting one. Conrad does not define it in the above short quotation or in the crucial pages of which it forms part. We know only that scepticism is far more than mere distrust of priests and that lack of it betrays the masses. We can trace its meaning, however, in Nostromo's thought. For as he reflects bitterly upon his fate, he feels increasingly that Signora Teresa (may God have her soul) was right. He, Nostromo, had never been taken into account. He had been used like a pawn in a game. He who had unquestioningly worked for the mine ('Nostromo here and Nostromo there—where is Nostromo?—Nostromo can do this and that' [417])—behold, he had found himself a traitor under the new régime. The simple fact of popular approval, which had been his driving force up to the moment, was no longer there. His way of life, his belief in himself and in the mine he served, had been taken from him. 'In the downfall of all the realities that made his force', he fell back on superstition, sensing in the sinister call of the owl the certainty of Teresa's death and of his own betrayal (418).

A thorough-going sceptic would not have been overcome in this way. He would not have placed faith in the adulation of men and women or in the stability of the mine. He would have trusted no aspect of life, any more than Conrad himself trusted the calm blue sea which he had so often seen turn into a frenzied one. A sceptic is always aware that men (including himself) are insignificant; that they are 'swallowed up in the immensity of things' (501). That most men do, in fact, take seriously all sorts of human activity is simply self-deception. A true sceptic does not believe in the value even of his own feelings. Nostromo's tragedy is that he *has* believed in himself—in his attractiveness to women and in his worth to the great mine. After the night on the gulf, he can believe in these things no longer:

> The confused and intimate impressions of universal dissolution which beset a subjective nature at any strong check to its ruling passion had a bitterness approaching that of death itself. He was simple. He was as ready to become the prey of any belief, superstition, or desire as a child.   417

In these pages Conrad's prose rhythms and vivid images dramatise with great intensity Nostromo's despair. It is with extreme bitterness that the Capataz realises that the only man who cares about his fate is Decoud. He has never understood Decoud—how could he, when Decoud had that complete scepticism which he himself lacked? He senses the fact without comprehending it. That is why he has always felt 'vaguely uneasy' in Decoud's presence.

There is no misunderstanding Decoud. He admits that editing *Porvenir* is 'not a serious occupation' (177), and declares that friendship between man and woman is an impossibility. As far as a man can regard life as meaningless, Decoud does. The one inconsistency in his attitude is his love for Antonia, which is the cause of his work for the mine and its silver.

For all this, Decoud is just as vulnerable to life as Nostromo. Conrad is careful to leave the reader in no doubt about this. When Decoud first appears we are told that he has 'pushed universal raillery to a point when it blinded him to the genuine impulses of his own nature' (153). Again, we are told that when he is with Nostromo attempting to save the silver, the darkness of the night 'deprived him of the only weapon he could use with effect'—his intelligence (275). Alone on the Great Isabel, Decoud has been placed in a situation which tests his scepticism to the utmost. To ensure that the reader cannot miss the point, there are both the vivid concrete details of the scene and Conrad's comments on it. Bereft of all reason for living, however mistaken it might have been, Decoud does not wish to live. He dies, Conrad says, 'from solitude and want of faith in himself and others' (496). The crucial paragraph of this section runs as follows:

> He spent the night open-eyed, and when the day broke he ate something with the same indifference. The brilliant 'Son Decoud', the spoiled darling of the family, the lover of Antonia and the journalist of Sulaco, was not fit to grapple with himself single-handed. Solitude from mere outward condition of existence becomes very swiftly a state of soul in which the affectations of irony and scepticism have no place. It takes possession of the mind, and drives forth the thought into the exile of utter unbelief. After three days of waiting for the sight of some human face, Decoud caught himself entertaining a doubt of his own individuality. It had merged into the world of cloud and water, of natural forces and forms of nature. In our activity alone do we find the sustaining illusion of an independent existence as against the whole scheme of things of which we form a helpless part. Decoud lost all belief in the reality of his action past and to come. On the fifth day an immense melancholy descended upon him palpably. He resolved not to give himself up to these people in Sulaco, who had beset him, unreal and terrible, like jibbering and obscene spectres. He saw himself struggling feebly in their midst, and Antonia, gigantic and lovely like an allegorical statue, looking on with scornful eyes at his weakness.   497–8

If, then, Nostromo's simple faith in things is inadequate to withstand the blows of fate, so equally is Decoud's total scepticism. What attitude, we may ask, is possible between the two extremes? Heyst's father on his death-bed points the way, bitter though his words are. He is replying to his son's appeal for guidance in the living of his own life:

> 'You still believe in something, then?' he said in a clear voice, which had been growing feeble of late.
>
> 'You believe in flesh and blood perhaps? A full and equable contempt would soon do away with that, too. But since you have not attained to it, I advise you to cultivate that form of contempt which is called pity. It is perhaps the least difficult—always remembering that you, too, if you are anything, are as pitiful as the rest, yet never expecting any pity for yourself.'
>
> VICTORY, 174

This is like an observation made by Conrad in a review of a
now forgotten book, *The Ascending Effort* by George Bourne.
Many a man, he claims, believes that the earth goes round the
sun, and that it is really no more than 'one small blob of mud
among several others, spinning ridiculously with a waggling
motion like a top about to fall'. But, he adds, 'while watching a
sunset he sheds his belief; he sees the sun as a small and useful
object, the servant of his needs and the witness of his ascending
efforts . . .' So, part of a man believes in the Copernican system,
though, in general, he lives by the Ptolemaic system, with
himself, and the earth he inhabits, at the centre of things. It is
the same with scepticism. A man may have an intensely sceptical
outlook, but as a participant in the field of human action he
will often be touched by pity and compassion.

It is an attitude that finds quiet expression in the novels.
Conrad has not the deliberate pessimism of a Hardy nor the
fierce protest at human nature that belonged to Swift. He is
content to record what are for him the universal conditions of
life. Men, he thinks, are well advised to adopt the armour of
scepticism, even though they cannot do so wholly. For the rest,
it is best to look with sympathy and pity on human behaviour.

'Warmness of heart' and 'largeness of sympathy' are expressions that occur regularly in Conrad's reviews of the work of
other writers. They, or words very similar, will be found in the
essays on Henry James, Anatole France, Turgenev and Stephen
Crane. 'The sight of human affairs', said Conrad in the familiar
Preface to *A Personal Record*, 'deserves admiration and pity. . . .
Resignation, not mystic, not detached, but resignation open-
eyed, conscious and informed by love, is the only one of our
feelings for which it is impossible to become a sham' (xix).

THE FUTILITY OF ANARCHY: 'THE SECRET AGENT'
In *The Secret Agent* Conrad continues his depiction of men in
society. This time we are in a world of spying and counter-
spying, of government departments and police action. It is
accorded an unfailing irony which has no place for the love-

interest which softens both *Nostromo* and *Under Western Eyes*; it has a muted violence and pointlessness which is as terrifying in its own way as the world of *Heart of Darkness*.

There is the Secret Agent himself, Mr. Verloc. It is his boast that he has had his finger on every 'murdering plot for the last eleven years'; he has treacherously sent off scores of revolutionists 'with their bombs in their blamed pockets to get themselves caught on the frontier' (238). Chief Inspector Heat of the English police admits that Verloc's information very likely saved 'ugly trouble' on the day of an Imperial visit to London (129). He is, in fact, a *double* agent working for both sides. Now, with the coming of a new First Secretary in the Foreign Embassy which employs him, Mr. Verloc finds himself ordered to blow up Greenwich Observatory. His life as a 'rather well-known hanger-on and emissary of the Revolutionary Red Committee' (130) is not to be so easy in the future. It is a long time since he served the five-year sentence which earned him his reputation as an anarchist. Since his release he has sent his reports and sheltered behind his ownership of a shop selling mildly pornographic literature. 'By a mystic accord of temperament and necessity, [he] had been set apart to be a secret agent all his life' (180). The truth is that he is thoroughly bourgeois at heart. 'His repose and his security' are his dearest possessions, and his two strongest instincts are 'conventional respectability' and 'dislike of all kinds of recognised labour' (52–3). As he notes this, Conrad permits himself a finely ironic sentence: 'For obviously one does not revolt against the advantages and opportunities of the state, but against the price which must be paid for the same in the coin of accepted morality, self-restraint, and toil'.

The other revolutionists are just as compromised. Mr. Verloc, 'with the insight of a kindred temperament', knows all about them. They meet at his shop. Karl Yundt, supposed terrorist, is lazy, swaggering and selfish, a posturing shadow. Michaelis, annexed by a wealthy old lady and writing his worthless and sprawling memoirs, has replaced prison life by 'mooning about in shady lanes for days together in a delicious and humanitarian idleness'. Ossipon will want for nothing 'as long as there are silly girls with savings-bank books in the world' (52–3). They have one ability in common—they can talk largely, abstractly and fluently of capitalism and anarchy, of the service of humanity, of *The Corroding Vices of the Middle Class* (this last is the title of a pamphlet by Comrade Ossipon). This is the bright lot to whom Conrad introduces us in the third chapter, immediately after Mr. Vladimir's outline to Verloc of his bomb-throwing philosophy. As the Professor says of them: 'Their character is built upon conventional morality. It leans on the social order'. They are 'worthy delegates for revolutionary propaganda', as unable to think 'as any respectable grocer or journalist of them all' (68).

The Professor is the only revolutionary we can admire. Chapters IV and V are given over to him and his fanatical ambition to destroy public faith in legality by some form of collective or individual violence. When Ossipon asks him what he is aiming at, he replies curtly: 'the perfect detonator'. Ossipon, finding this too much for his normal thinking, makes a face. The Professor sees and interprets the grimace, commenting that to want to revolutionise the existing social order is to be its slave; the only thing is to destroy it. He tells Ossipon with great scorn:

> 'You might ask the police for a testimonial of good conduct. They know where every one of you slept last night. Perhaps if you asked them they would consent to publish some sort of official statement.'   77

And off he goes, grasping lightly in his pocket the india-rubber ball which contains the detonator with which he can at any moment end his own life as well as the lives of all those near him.

What we admire in the Professor is his single-mindedness, his freedom from the selfish cant of the other revolutionaries, from whom he keeps himself loftily aloof. But he is just as deluded as they are. His ability to see the true nature of the world, with its 'artificial, corrupt and blasphemous' morality, does not prevent him from seeking in 'vengeful bitterness' the 'appearances of power and personal prestige'. Conrad comments:

> and in their own way the most ardent of revolutionaries are
> perhaps doing no more but seeking for peace in common with
> the rest of mankind—the peace of soothed vanity, of satisfied
> appetites, or perhaps of appeased conscience.   81

Talking about the novel in this way may give the impression
that it is concerned with ideas rather than with people. The truth
is that it is organised as a succession of scenes, each of which
throws a light on revolutionary activity. When, for example,
the Professor leaves Ossipon, he accidentally meets Chief
Inspector Heat. It is a splendidly handled incident. The Professor has left the busy main street, partly through doubt of his
or anyone's ability to move the mass of mankind. He is happier
alone, and goes along a narrow and dark alley. Its abandoned
houses and seedy second-hand furniture store form a fitting
background for his meeting with a guardian of the society which
has produced them. Each man appreciates the other's position.
Lonely and removed from the bustle of the City they converse
warily. At this point Conrad interpolates as a gruesome flash-
back the scene where Heat examines the fragmentary human
remains of the Greenwich explosion. Since it is the Professor's
dynamite that has produced this 'heap of nameless fragments',
his words take on an appallingly sinister aspect.

Inspector Heat cannot understand anarchists as he can
burglars.

> As a matter of fact, the mind and instincts of a burglar are of
> the same kind as the mind and instincts of a police officer. Both
> recognise the same conventions, and have a working knowledge
> of each other's methods and of the routine of their trades.   92

He contents himself with warning the Professor that he knows
where to find him. The reply is a threat of annihilation involving
'the unpleasantness of being buried together with me, though
I suppose your friends would make an effort to sort us out as
much as possible'. (The ironic flavour of the book is in these
words, contrasting the mild 'unpleasantness' with the atrocious
sentiment it characterises.) The threat causes the sounds and
images of the city life around Heat to appear maddeningly

desirable to him, though as a brave and effective man he gives as good as he gets in the verbal duel. The two separate to continue what the Professor scornfully calls 'the game'—the necessary moves and counter-moves of lawlessness and legality. 'Lunatic', Heat mutters, as he thinks of the Professor (93–7).

In the world of *The Secret Agent*, however, this judgment cannot be taken at face value. People are lunatic partly because 'the game' has made them so. The novel adopts throughout the method of inviting the reader to turn normal judgments upside down. In the opening pages, for instance, the interview between Verloc and Mr. Vladimir has its lunatic aspects.

Vladimir suggests conversing in French and promptly rattles off highly idiomatic English; Verloc alternately orates in a great bass voice and murmurs huskily; he demonstrates the power of his voice (the secret of his one-time hold over the masses) by opening the window, calling 'constable' above the roar of London and scaring the wits out of a policeman below (24). There are very many such incongruities throughout the book.

In an important way, the half-witted Stevie represents normality. Karl Yundt's absurd talk 'about eating people's flesh and drinking blood' makes Stevie quite simply afraid, as do many of Ossipon's tracts. His mother's reaction is to regret that he ever went to school, the implication being that he would have been better off unable to read (59–60).

This brings us to another aspect of the novel. 'From a certain point of view', says the Assistant Commissioner, 'we are in the presence of a domestic drama' (222). It is a drama conditioned by, and throwing light on, 'the game' played by society. Verloc, for instance, loves his wife as his 'chief possession'; to him 'the sacredness of domestic peace' is founded on a view of his wife as a piece of property (179). He sees Stevie in the way a man not particularly fond of animals looks on 'his wife's beloved cat' (39). And once he has been harassed by Mr. Vladimir he shuts himself off completely from those he lives with. Between his job and his personal life there is no real connection. (At home, he eats with his hat pushed off his forehead as though he is in a public restaurant.)

Mrs. Verloc is the counterpart of the Professor, another fanatical pursuer of a fixed idea—in her case, the welfare of Stevie, her half-witted brother. It is to provide a home for him that she has married the lodger, Adolf Verloc, instead of the young butcher whom she 'loved dearly', but whose father 'threatened to kick him out of the business if he made such a fool of himself as to marry a girl with a crippled mother and a crazy idiot of a boy on her hands'—an attitude to marriage very like Verloc's own, it may be noted (275–6). Ironically, Conrad invests her remarks to Stevie with genuine tenderness, while making her address her husband with routine placidity— 'You'll catch cold walking about in your socks like this' (177). Beyond her mother and brother, she has no vision, feeling profoundly 'that things do not stand much looking into' (241). The result is that after murdering Verloc she grotesquely misunderstands the intentions of Ossipon, and, after the desertion of this supposed 'radiant messenger of life' (274), commits suicide by jumping off a cross-Channel boat.

Stevie is even more a victim. His naïveté has a Garden of Eden quality which cannot be accommodated in a world of Vladimirs, Ossipons and Sir Ethelreds. 'Bad world for poor people', he mutters, though he has faith that the police will mend matters. He is surprised when his sister tells him that the police 'aren't for that'.

> 'What are they for then, Winn? What are they for? Tell me.'
>
> 'Don't you know what the police are for, Stevie? They are there so that them as have nothing shouldn't take anything away from them who have.'   173

His death is really the penalty exacted by 'the game' for his too-trusting spirit. The book's repeated misunderstandings reach their ironic climax in Verloc's remark as his wife silently contemplates the death of Stevie, the truth about which she has just learned: 'Do be reasonable, Winnie. What would it have been if you had lost me?' (234). And we may note in passing that it is the measure of Conrad's technical advance that the germ of this scene is to be found in the unconvincing early short story, *The Return*.

The Secret Agent offers plenty of scope to a Marxist critic for analysis as an exposure of what E. M. Forster said he himself belonged to—'the fag-end of Victorian liberalism'. Certainly the basic attitude behind this novel can be matched by that of others—the eroding action of the 'material interests' represented by the mine in *Nostromo*, the sorry farce of the financial dealings in *Chance*, the grim analysis of the liquidation of the Tropical Belt Company at the start of *Victory*, and the sordid exploitation of the natives in *Heart of Darkness*. All these offer plenty of evidence that Conrad, coming late to a settled life on shore, viewed cynically industrial society and the sources of its wealth. During his active life as a sailor he had experienced the purposeful unity of crews whose aims were not individual gain, but the completion of voyages over the great oceans of the world. Small wonder, in view of this background, that he had little sympathy with what he called 'the unnatural mysteries of the financial world'. Many critics since D. H. Lawrence have complained that Galsworthy began *The Forsyte Saga* by satirising the tyranny of property and wealth in capitalist England, and ended by condoning them. Of course, Galsworthy's roots were in the very society he at first condemned, as Conrad's were not. Perhaps it was his alien origin which enabled Conrad to sense almost prophetically the growing violence of the twentieth century. *The Secret Agent* was written seven years before the First World War. Yet it contains the words, supposedly uttered on his deathbed by Mr. Vladimir's predecessor—

> Unhappy Europe! Thou shalt perish by the moral insanity of thy children! 28

It would nevertheless be a misreading of *The Secret Agent* to interpret it as an anti-capitalist novel. It happens, as a work of art, to present us with a grim picture of a world given over to the worship of materialistic values. People, Mr. Vladimir argues at the start, believe 'in some mysterious way [that] science is at the source of their material prosperity' (33). That is why he suggests an attack on Greenwich Observatory, the symbol of scientific progress. At the end of the novel, the Professor and Ossipon are discussing the role of science in the future. But Ossipon is so oppressed with the guilt of his part in Mrs. Verloc's death that he feels his approaching ruin. And the Professor cannot get rid of the thought of 'a mankind as numerous as the sands of the seashore, as indestructible, as difficult to handle' (306). (The same thought comforts Inspector Heat [144].) If he dared to formulate a clear statement it would be to the effect that in a mankind which 'does not know what it wants' mediocrity will always win. The world will continue like the mechanical piano in the Silenus beer-hall, rowdy, abrupt and meaningless. 'This world of ours is not such a very serious affair after all' (150), are words Conrad uses (in his own voice as author) about the Assistant Commissioner's pleasant interference in the Greenwich affair. Uttered with grim stoicism, they could well be the reader's too.

The Secret Agent is Conrad's most successful novel. In all the others, even *Nostromo* which is greater, it is possible to point to technical faults or weaknesses. Only here the ironic mask never slips, the artistic vision, bleak though it is, is not flawed.

FROM WITHDRAWAL TO COMPASSION: 'UNDER WESTERN EYES'

One of Conrad's letters refers to the *The Secret Agent's* concern with the worthlessness and baseness of men. The later novels look less bleakly on human wickedness. Their heroes try to avoid involvement with others, fail to do so, but learn through their failure to exercise compassion.

Razumov in *Under Western Eyes* lives to this pattern. The illegitimate son of an aristocrat, he is without family. 'No home influences had shaped his opinions or feelings. He was as lonely in the world as a man swimming in the deep sea'. For him, his own name was a mere word, a 'label of solitary individuality' (10). He does not so much choose detachment from life as find it forced upon him. He shrinks mentally from the fray of the world 'as a good-natured man may shrink from taking definite sides in a violent family quarrel'. His ambition is high academic success, the gaining of a silver medal and perhaps even of a professorship. With dramatic effect and fine irony, Conrad shows Razumov climbing the stairs to his own room as he day-dreams of an announcement in the papers that he is this year's silver medallist. 'This is but a shadow', he says to himself (14). It is indeed. When he enters his room a moment later, it is to find the murderer, Haldin, asking for his help. Razumov has found involvement thrust upon him.

After agonising uncertainty, Razumov betrays Haldin to the Tsarist authorities. Strangely, he does so in such a way as to win the confidence of both the revolutionaries and the police. He is sent to Geneva by the former, though he is in truth an agent of the latter. In Geneva, he meets Haldin's mother and sister. Little by little the facts about Haldin's death are brought to light, and Razumov's security is threatened. Luckily for him, the wrong construction is put on them and the obscure figure of a coachman (Ziemianitch) is blamed. Razumov, it seems, is now safe.

He hurries to Miss Haldin with the story of Ziemianitch's treachery only to find that she does not trust him. It is then he realises that in giving up Haldin he has betrayed himself. Without realising what has been happening, he has fallen in love with Haldin's sister. It is she who has been 'tearing him to pieces and dragging the secret for ever to his lips . . . appointed to undo the evil by making him betray himself back into truth and peace' (358). So far, the theme—the working out of a moral fault—looks back to *Lord Jim*.

Now comes a new note, first encountered in Tekla, the old *dame de compagnie*, whom Razumov meets at Mme. S's where the revolutionaries gather. She tells him her story (147 ff.). She has spent much time looking after a revolutionary who had cut himself off from all friends because he had under torture revealed secrets (a return to the Dr. Monygham theme in *Nostromo*). This fault the poor man looked on as inexpiable, and he 'crept into a hole to bear his remorse stoically'. There Tekla had looked after him devotedly until he died. To the end he had remained uncomforted, even though he had been found by understanding comrades who never 'dreamed of reproaching him with his indiscretion before the police'. His fate had filled Tekla with hatred for all political bodies. At the time of meeting Razumov she is living in the hope of 'seeing all the Ministries destroyed'. It is a naïveté which represents the best in the revolutionaries— the virtue of compassion. She exercises it again at the end of the book when she devotes herself to looking after the maimed Razumov 'unweariedly with the pure joy of unselfish devotion' (379).

Miss Haldin follows her lead. After the death of her mother she spends her time working amongst 'the horrors of over-crowded jails and the heart-rending misery of bereaved homes' (378). Once or twice she speaks openly of her hopes for the world if people will only grow more loving. This is not a lapse into sentimentality, for her strength and innocence give her the right to say it:

> 'I must own to you that I shall never give up looking forward to the day when all discord shall be silenced . . . there must be many bitter hours! But at last anguish of hearts shall be extinguished in love.'
> 376

'VICTORY'

Victory develops along parallel lines. Heyst, its hero, chooses to protect himself from the blows of fate in a special way. Warned by his dying father to 'Look on, make no sound', he formulates an unusual defence against life. His method is:

> . . . a solitary achievement, accomplished not by a hermit-like withdrawal with its silence and immobility, but by a system of restless wandering, by the detachment of an impermanent dweller amongst changing scenes. In this scheme he had perceived the means of passing through life without suffering and almost without a single care in the world—invulnerable because elusive.
> 90

Like Razumov, he fails to keep apart from the life of others. He has no sooner reached the conclusion that 'he who forms a tie is lost' (the 'germ of corruption' having entered his soul), than he befriends Morrison. It is not an action forced on him, like Razumov's decision to betray Haldin; it is the result of 'a moment of inadvertence' (199–200).

As it happens, Morrison dies. Heyst is able to settle more firmly than ever into his life of detachment. Then, for a second time, he allows himself to become involved with someone else's problems. He comes across a girl (Lena) who is obviously being victimised. The fact of her misery so impresses itself on him that his abstract theory succumbs to the living reality: he could not defend himself from his compassion; 'his sceptical mind was dominated by the fulness of his heart' (83). The upshot is that, like Captain Anthony in *Chance*, he takes the girl away.

Her action in trusting Heyst is quite innocent—'without a sense of guilt, in a desire for safety and from a profound need of placing her trust where her woman's instinct guided her ignorance' (95). Soon after they have arrived on their island retreat, Lena astonishes Heyst by pleading with him to love her for what she is. Ironically, he has just been reading his father's words: 'of the stratagems of life the most cruel is the consolation of love—the most subtle, too; for the desire is the bed of dreams'. With her appeal, all Heyst's defences are broken: 'Life has him fairly by the throat'. He comforts himself with the reflection that they are cut off from the world. He and Lena will have time to learn the lessons of love—'nothing can break in on us here' (219–23).

He has no sooner said this than the Chinese servant announces that he has seen a boat with three white men in it. Yet again, Heyst has to act within the entanglements of human relationships. All he had wanted was to be left alone with Lena. Now this is impossible. He is also keenly aware of his responsiblity for her. 'He no longer belongs to himself'; Lena represents a call 'imperious and august'—he must guard her at all costs (245).

The novel seems to be saying that this is the only way in which men can love—by submitting to the loved one's call on their loyalties. Heyst can do this as other Conrad heroes cannot because he has been guilty of no moral lapse. The story becomes a stark struggle between Heyst and Lena on the one hand and the infamous trio on the other. Lena sees the issues more plainly than Heyst. From the moment Ricardo breaks into her privacy, she thinks of him as 'the embodied evil of the world' (298). The knowledge enables her to face danger with feminine duplicity and immense courage. She gives her life to save his. Heyst fails at first to understand her sacrifice. When he does, he kills himself in remorse.

Writing an appreciation of Henry James in the year he wrote *Victory*, Conrad stated:

> That a sacrifice must be made, that something has to be given up, is the truth engraved in the innermost recesses of the fair temple built for our edification by the masters of fiction. There is no other secret behind the curtain. All adventure, all love, every success is resumed in the supreme energy of an act of renunciation. It is the uttermost limit of our power; it is the most potent and effective force at our disposal on which rest the labours of a solitary man in his study, the rock on which have been built commonwealths whose might casts a dwarfing shadow upon two oceans. Like a natural force which is obscured as much as illuminated by the multiplicity of phenomena, the power of renunciation is obscured by the mass of weaknesses, vacillations, secondary motives and false steps and compromises which make up the sum of our activity. But no man or woman worthy of the name, can pretend to anything more, to anything greater.

It is a rather grandiose statement (and contains a typical Gallicism in the word 'resumed', meaning 'summed up'), but its intention is clear. Conrad is confessing his faith in the sacrifice made by one human being for another. To this faith *Victory* is his best testimony.

Chance, already considered from a different viewpoint on pp. 85–88 and written between *Under Western Eyes* and *Victory*, is another variation on the theme of compassionate action. Its hero and heroine are both lonely and meaningless until they meet each other and set about learning Heyst's lesson of love. When, at the end of the novel, Captain Anthony dies, the lesson is about to begin again, this time between Flora and young Powell.

The Rover (1923), Conrad's last completed novel, continues the theme. Peyrol, its hero, is no worse for having been a member of the illegal Brotherhood of the Coast: his was 'a sincere lawlessness' (209). He retires to end his days near the sea, quiet and unnoticed. He has more right than Heyst to his cut off life because he has already lived so fully. Inevitably, however, he becomes part of his new community. Without meaning to, he brings fresh hope to the village cripple and to simple Michel. Ultimately, he deliberately sacrifices his life for the twin causes of the French nation and of the young couple, Réal and Arlette. 'One could talk a long time of him', said his friend the cripple by way of epitaph (285). In the book's last sentence, the country he served so well takes a noble leave of him:

> The breath of the evening breeze came to cool the heated rocks of Escampobar; and the mulberry tree, the only big tree on the head of the peninsula, standing like a sentinel at the gate of the yard, sighed faintly in a shudder of all its leaves as if regretting the Brother of the Coast, the man of dark deeds, but of large heart, who often at noonday would lie down to sleep under its shade. 286

THE LAST NOVELS; ARTISTIC DECLINE

The title page of *The Rover* bears the epigraph 'Sleep after Toyle'. It speaks for Conrad as well as for his hero, Peyrol. Both as writer and man he was getting tired.

Critics have not agreed about when the tiredness and artistic decline began. Some consider *Victory* (1915) an impressive novel. F. R. Leavis praises it highly in *The Great Tradition*. Others think it a marked falling-off from *Nostromo* and *The Secret Agent*. Douglas Hewitt states this case well in *Joseph Conrad. A reassessment* (1952). Each reader must decide for himself.

There are, however, certain features common to the novels written after *Chance* (1913). They are less involved technically and are therefore easier to understand; they have many fabular elements; and they are much concerned with love and sacrifice. On the other hand, their relatively simple subjects and manner are accompanied by a dangerous softening in Conrad's attitude to life. This may have been connected with the anxiety of the 1914–18 war. It appears most clearly in the sentimentality of the heroines (see p. 72) and in the clichés of the often tired prose. It is at its worst in *The Tale* (*Tales of Hearsay* 1916) and in *The Arrow of Gold* (1918). This last, told autobiographically and set against a background of illicit gun-running, is a romantically sentimental and over-dramatised treatment of a young man's first love affair. It is best forgotten.

The Rescue (1919) was a return to the Malayan world of the first novels. It depicts the youthful Lingard who has allowed the course of his life to be altered by the claims of a native prince and princess whom he has befriended. His efforts for them fail because, when the yacht of a wealthy English couple runs aground at the very scene of his activities, he falls in love with the yacht owner's wife. But the working-out is too careful and leisurely. The story moves at an unvarying speed, so that the reader is too conscious of its classic correctness of form. The style, too, lacks variety. There are good things in it—the character of old Jorgensen and the married life of the Travers. But it is, in Conrad's own words, 'slightly inflated'. Its grandiose air overcomes but cannot fascinate the reader.

Suspense was the novel Conrad was working on when he died. It deals with the period of Napoleon's exile in Elba. As it stands, it is portentously slow-moving—far more so than *The Rescue*. It is a final illustration of artistic decline.

CONCLUSION

It is hard to fit Conrad into any history of the English novel. He has no forebears and no obvious successors.

Yet the general tenor of his work is fairly clear. Like James, he took his chosen art form with great seriousness. The subject of his novels is quite simply man and his place in the created world. Conrad's characters are imprisoned in the fundamental isolation of every human being and try desperately in an unconcerned universe to give their lives meaning. They struggle passionately against their condition. Those that can, live out the simple virtues of loyalty, discipline and hard work by devoting themselves to the limited end of sailing a ship and doing the job nearest to hand. The rest are caught in the quicksands of men's unending capacity for imagining for themselves more glory and success than they can ever achieve. Almayer, Lord Jim, Nostromo and Razumov all see the failure of the projected lives which their imaginations had dreamed of.

The causes of their failure are hidden deep in man's nature. It is not just Trollope that seems simple beside Conrad. Even the far greater George Eliot does. She depicts a world whose moral values are clear and can be used to measure her characters accordingly. Conrad, with his exploration of the dark side of human nature, does not. His novels are full of depths and uncertainties which he wrestled with but could not fully understand—otherwise *Lord Jim* and *Nostromo* would have been clearer novels. And it has to be admitted that his struggle to explore them often led to wordiness and to the over-elaboration of an already elaborate technique. They are the faults of a serious endeavour to tackle a serious problem, of a determination to avoid the conventional manner which will suit only conventional material.

It is the mark of the Conrad hero that he withers into truth. If he is like Nostromo, a superb unthinking animal, he falls from grace as soon as he is divorced from his customary surroundings. Decoud, Dr. Monygham and the more imaginative characters, on the other hand, are made by circumstances to look sadly on the myriad illusions which are the conditions of human existence.

Conrad's extraordinarily varied art is a search for greater awareness. As he himself said (in the Author's Note to *Typhoon*), in the end every novel must 'justify itself in its own way to the conscience of each successive reader'.

Bibliography

There are many critical studies of Conrad. This short list suggests some introductory reading.

GENERAL

Miriam Allott: *Novelists on the Novel* (Routledge & Kegan Paul, 1959).

J. Warren Beach: *The Twentieth Century Novel* (Century Co., 1932).

Wayne Booth: *The Rhetoric of Fiction* (Univ. of Chicago, 1961).

Ford Madox Ford: *The English Novel from the Earliest Days to the Death of Joseph Conrad* (Constable, 1930).

Ford Madox Ford: *Thus to Revisit* (Chapman & Hall, 1921).

Henry James: *The Art of the Novel*, ed. by R. P. Blackmur (C. Scribner's Sons, 1935).

Henry James: *The Art of Fiction* (Oxford, 1948).

F. R. Leavis: *The Great Tradition* (Chatto & Windus, 1948).

Katherine Lever: *The Novel and the Reader* (Methuen, 1961).

CONRAD'S LIFE AND LETTERS

Ford Madox Ford: *Joseph Conrad: A Personal Rememberance* (Duckworth, 1924).

Ford Madox Ford: *Return to Yesterday* (Victor Gollancz, 1931).

E. Garnett (ed.): *Letters from Conrad 1895–1924* (Nonesuch, 1928).

G. Jean-Aubry: *Joseph Conrad: Life and Letters*, 2 vols. (Heinemann, 1927).

B. Russell: *Portraits from Memory* (Allen & Unwin, 1956).

CRITICAL

W. Allen: *The English Novel*, chap. 6, section 6 (Penguin, 1962).

J. Baines: *Joseph Conrad: a Critical Biography* (Weidenfeld & Nicolson, 1960).

J. D. Gordan: *Joseph Conrad. The Making of a Novelist* (Harvard, 1940).

D. Hewitt: *Joseph Conrad. A Reassessment* (Bowes & Bowes, 1952).

F. R. Karl: *A Reader's Guide to Joseph Conrad* (Thames & Hudson, 1960).

N. Sherry: *Conrad's Eastern World* (Cambridge, 1966).

T. Tanner: *Conrad: Lord Jim* (Arnold, 1963).

Index

Conrad's Works

General